Praise for *Mentoring and Coaching: A Lifeline for Teachers in a Multicultural Setting*

"The authors take an important multicultural approach to mentoring by showing how teachers from different cultural heritages translate concepts into practices. Their concrete examples at different grade levels explain how struggling teachers can become successful. Easy to read and understand, this book contains valuable resources, self-assessment tools, and tips for effective communication that will ensure successful implementation of mentoring programs."

—Ann Nevin
Professor Emerita
Arizona State University

"In this book you hear the voices of new teachers who have struggled with the myriad of challenges that drive so many good and potentially effective teachers out of a career in education. Mentoring and coaching have made a difference in the professional lives of many motivated and talented teachers who have, in turn, improved the learning outcomes of their students. Gudwin and Salazar-Wallace provide a realistic and practical guide to successful mentoring and coaching that is grounded in their own successful experiences with struggling teachers and students."

—Ronald Felton
Associate Director
Urban Special Education Leadership Collaborative

"Sustaining young, spirited, gifted teachers in our public schools, especially in our urban systems, is one of our country's greatest challenges in education. This book, written by two educators who have brilliantly faced that challenge and helped create a comprehensive program to retain those teachers, is a blueprint for the nation's 'way out' of losing the very people who can inspire a higher level of academic achievement for our children."

—Joan T. Wynne
Professor and Associate Director
Center for Urban Education & Innovation
Florida International University

"Using the voices of teachers, mentors, and school leaders, this book is an insightful analysis of the role that mentoring and teacher induction programs play in the retention and success of urban public school teachers. A must-read for all stakeholders serious about teacher success in today's challenged climate surrounding public education. This book represents the hope that is necessary to retain the next generation of public school teachers."

—Louie F. Rodriguez, EdD
Assistant Professor
Educational Leadership and Curriculum College of Education
California State University

MENTORING

AND

COACHING

A Lifeline

for Teachers

in a

MULTICULTURAL SETTING

DENISE M. GUDWIN
MAGDA D. SALAZAR-WALLACE

Foreword by Joan T. Wynne

CORWIN
A SAGE Company

For information:

Corwin
A SAGE Company
2455 Teller Road
Thousand Oaks, California 91320
(800) 233-9936
Fax: (800) 417-2466
www.corwinpress.com

SAGE India Pvt. Ltd.
B 1/I 1 Mohan Cooperative
    Industrial Area
Mathura Road, New Delhi 110 044
India

SAGE Ltd.
1 Oliver's Yard
55 City Road
London EC1Y 1SP
United Kingdom

SAGE Asia-Pacific Pte. Ltd.
33 Pekin Street #02-01
Far East Square
Singapore 048763

Printed in the United States of America

Library of Congress Cataloging-in-Publication Data

Gudwin, Denise M.
Mentoring and coaching: a lifeline for teachers in a multicultural setting/Denise M. Gudwin and Magda D. Salazar-Wallace; foreword by Joan T. Wynne.
        p. cm.
Includes bibliographical references and index.
ISBN 978-1-4129-7957-3 (cloth)
ISBN 978-1-4129-7958-0 (pbk.)

    1. Multicultural education—Florida—Dade County. 2. Education, Bilingual—Florida—Dade County. 3. Teachers—Training of—Florida—Dade County. 4. Mentoring—Florida—Dade County. 5. Personal coaching—Florida—Dade County. 6. Peer review—Florida—Dade County. I. Salazar-Wallace, Magda D. II. Title.

LC1099.4.F6G83 2010
370.71'55—dc22   2009028158

This book is printed on acid-free paper.

09 10 11 12 13   10 9 8 7 6 5 4 3 2 1

Acquisitions Editor:	Dan Alpert
Associate Editor:	Megan Bedell
Production Editor:	Jane Haenel
Copy Editor:	Claire Larson
Typesetter:	C&M Digitals (P) Ltd.
Proofreader:	Cheryl Rivard
Indexer:	Sylvia Coates
Cover and Graphic Designer:	Michael Dubowe

Contents

List of Tables and Figures

TABLES

FIGURES

Foreword

Sustaining young, spirited, gifted teachers in our public schools, especially in our urban systems, is one of our country's greatest challenges in education. This book, written by two educators who have brilliantly faced that challenge and helped create a comprehensive program to retain those teachers, is a blueprint for the nation's "way out" of losing the very people who can inspire a higher level of academic achievement for our children.

This text substantiates what Asa G. Hilliard III, educator, psychologist, and historian, insisted was necessary for the promotion of powerful teaching. Dr. Hilliard said,

> Revolution, not reform, is required to release the power of teaching. . . . Virtually, all teachers possess tremendous power which can be released, given the proper exposure. We can't get to that point by tinkering with a broken system. We must change our intellectual structures, definitions and assumptions; then we can release teacher power. (1997)

Our large school systems are, indeed, broken. No quick fix or "tinkering" is going to work. The "fixes" offered in most charter schools and voucher systems have failed because they have ignored the lessons that Hilliard and these two practitioners hold to be true—that "proper exposure" of new teachers to expert professionals in the field and to democratic classroom philosophy and practices is essential. The hegemonic "structures" of institutional top-down leadership that privileges only the sons and daughters of the powerful elite demoralize all our teachers and keeps the nation's schools married to mind-numbing instruction and policies. The larger the system, the less it seems to challenge the racist and classist "definitions and assumptions" that constantly stifle the imaginations of the diverse populations of students who show up every day in classrooms across this nation. These policies and practices, however, are countered in the praxis advocated by Gudwin and Salazar-Wallace.

Unlike many other reform agents, these authors recognize the need and the methods for nurturing young professionals who work with our children in outdated and uncreative classrooms. They understand clearly the need to change the mindset of teachers who fall victim to society's notions that black, brown, and white children who are forced to live in poverty cannot academically excel. Gudwin and Salazar-Wallace create experiences for teachers to grapple with these societal myths and come to the other side— to a belief in the capacity of all children to soar when delivered a quality education. Understanding that all parents and communities bring wisdom to the table of education, the authors and the coaches teach their teachers how to encourage an honest reciprocity of knowledge-sharing in their classrooms. These teachers are coached to invite students and parents into the learning circle to enrich the curriculum and create culturally responsive pedagogy.

Mentoring and Coaching: A Lifeline for Teachers in a Multicultural Setting helps teachers and schools transcend the troubled waters of intellectual structures that have for too long trapped our professionals into practices that do not work for children or communities. As educational experts like Freire and Macedo (1987, p. 122) suggested decades ago, schools are never politically neutral. They either support the status quo or they create contexts where children learn to transform their worlds. Our teachers should be agents who can drive education beyond the boundaries of the status quo. If we are to push America toward the realization of its democratic promise for all people, not just for the power brokers, then we must develop teachers and schools that attend to liberation and transformation for everyone they serve. This is the "revolution" that Hilliard envisioned for our teachers. In fact, our democracy depends on the courage of our teachers to become co-creators in education for the liberation of children from all cultures and linguistic backgrounds.

As Bob Moses, Civil Rights legend, MacArthur Genius Fellow, and president of the Algebra Project, suggests, "All the children *in* the nation are the children *of* the nation" (2004). Our new teachers need the guidance of master teachers who understand the ramifications of that reality on the instructional philosophy and practices in their classrooms. This text can support that dialogue and praxis.

Moreover, this text is a rubric whose wisdom comes from real stories of real successes of collaboration between a large university and a giant urban school system in nurturing and mentoring beginning teachers so that they do the right thing for all the nation's children. Many of us are searching for effective induction plans for our teachers. Gudwin and Salazar-Wallace give us a "hands-on" model to guide us there.

Joan T. Wynne, PhD
Educational Leadership and Policy Studies
Florida International University
Miami, Florida

REFERENCES

Freire, Paulo, & Macedo, D. (1987). *Literacy*. New York: Bergin & Garvey.

Hilliard, Asa G., III. (1997). The structure of valid staff development. *Journal of Staff Development*, 18(2).

Moses, Bob. (2004). *Promotional video*. Miami: Center for Urban Education & Innovation at Florida International University.

Preface

Dear Educator,

We are happy to have this opportunity to share some wonderful success stories with you regarding working with new teachers. Whether you are a new teacher yourself or soon to be a new teacher, a **mentor** or master teacher, a school-site or central office administrator, a professional developer, an **instructional coach** or other school-site support personnel, or a university professor, you will gain practical knowledge linked to research and real-life stories that will positively impact the way you do business. Whether your area of expertise is early childhood, elementary, secondary, general education, special education, literacy, content, the arts, technical, foreign languages, or any other field of education, you will see a connecting thread in the lessons to be learned from stories shared, successes experienced, and struggles conquered in this book.

We also extend an invitation to you to replicate our work with new teachers—to add to your existing knowledge of induction, thereby expanding your own professional and personal growth and development.

As fellow colleagues and educators, we are excited to share great things about working with new teachers with you:

Chapter 1 provides you with an insight of our *mentoring experiences* and how mentoring positively affected our own personal and professional growth, which will help you in making the connections of successful mentoring. We will also reflect upon the characteristics of high-quality mentors.

Chapter 2 opens the door for you to get an insight on what a new teacher feels—and we will share with you the *voice of the struggling teacher*. We have much to learn from new teachers, if only we listen, really listen, to what they are and are not saying, and if we ask the right questions and provide the right level of support.

Chapter 3 delves into the concept of *teachers as leaders*, looking at personal experiences and characteristics, then taking us into *the role of the mentor*, and what we, as exemplary teachers, should do and how we should do it, with practical research and ideas that really work.

Chapter 4 provides you with the *characteristics of effective coaching*, with awareness of age, cultural, and linguistic differences as one of the highlights.

Chapter 5 shares the ins and outs of effective **communication** and its importance in working with new teachers.

Chapter 6 provides you a glimpse of an actual **case study**, featuring one particular program that excelled in supporting new teachers, with a 97% retention rate. This particular case study focused primarily on special education teachers with a small percentage of general education teachers. However, the content and concepts can be transferred easily to any group of teachers. It is not meant to be inclusive for only special education teachers, as that type of labeling would limit the readers' opportunities for replicating in any locale. The key? The commitment and passion apparent in the case study are woven into the necessary components of a highly successful program. We also discuss effective **induction programs** in general and what they should look like.

Chapter 7 focuses on quality **professional development** and how it can impact teachers, whether they are new to the field or seasoned mentors.

Chapter 8 enlightens you with *lessons learned* through the mentoring process, including tips on how to replicate one example of a successful program, as well as personal experiences shared by two new teachers.

Culturally and linguistically diverse (CLD) populations in most American schools are increasing—children from CLD heritages attend public school all over the United States, with an estimated 4.1 million students (8.5%) as English language learners (ELL) (Paige, 2004, p. 4). In Miami-Dade County Public Schools (M-DCPS), our district and the fourth largest school district in the nation, the ELL population is 52.5%. That's quite a difference from the 8.5% nationally! Our district has the largest minority student population in the state and is the only district in Florida where there are more minority teachers than white, non-Hispanic teachers (Florida Department of Education, 2007). The student population of this particular school system is composed of 9.6% white, non-Hispanic; 27.6% black, non-Hispanic; 60.4% Hispanic; and 2.4% other. The top ten foreign languages spoken by students in this school district are Spanish, Haitian Creole, French, Portuguese, Zhongwen (Chinese), Arabic, Russian, Urdu, Hebrew, and Vietnamese (Miami-Dade County Public Schools [M-DCPS], 2006b). Teachers face many challenges in teaching, but add to that the CLD factors, and the challenges can be overwhelming to a beginning teacher, especially when dealing with the barrier of communication of both students and parents.

Additionally, all teachers have new challenges, as children with disabilities are now receiving more and more instruction in general education classrooms due to current legislation, which requires them to have access to the general education curriculum, as well as students of diverse backgrounds. Added to the increased **diversity** of the children attending school is the continuing problem of lack of diversity in the current generation of teachers nationwide. Furthermore, in a summary of Pugach (2005), in Cochran-Smith and Zeichner (2005), "Despite the trend toward preparing prospective teachers to work with students with disabilities, few studies of program effects have been studied" (p. 25). Retention of beginning teachers and prevention of burnout continue to challenge public school personnel. A study conducted by the National Center for Education Statistics

(2005) shows that approximately 27.7% of new teachers leave the profession within the first three years, and in urban districts the attrition rate can jump to an alarming 30% to 50% in the first year. In the state of Florida, 11% of new graduates who taught in Florida public schools left the classroom after one year (Florida Department of Education, 2003). In M-DCPS (M-DCPS, 2006b), 17.3% of the teachers were new to the district; however, the teacher turnover rate in M-DCPS in 2005–2006 was 4.65%.

Increasing presence of mentoring programs for beginning teachers has resulted in an increase of teacher retention. In the past five years, M-DCPS has successfully implemented a beginning teacher program that has shown promising results in terms of retention. Our district sponsors numerous comprehensive teacher induction programs, one of which is a systematic structure of support for new and early-career special education teachers to assist them in becoming competent and effective professionals, focusing on mentor **teacher leader** partnerships and professional development for both the mentor teacher leaders and the new and early-career teachers. This particular program, Project GATE, a successful mentoring teacher induction program that was specifically designed for a particular group of teachers, in collaboration with a local state university and an urban school district, resulted in 97% retention of new and early-career special education teachers at the end of their first year, and is highlighted in Chapter 6. Brock and Grady (2007) suggest that such programs expect multiple outcomes such as retention of qualified teachers and enhanced professional growth.

Based upon both our personal and professional experiences, we anticipate sharing the successes of the new and early-career teachers and their mentors, despite the numerous challenges. We have effectively impacted their teaching practices, thereby creating a community of diverse learners that supported one another through various mentoring components. But besides all of that, something else occurred . . . there was a community formed, a family was established. As one new teacher reflects,

> It provided me a family of support; it was OK to cry, OK to get up one more day and do what I do. . . . I felt there was a sense of community; I had a sense of belonging. I didn't feel like a fish in a big ocean with nowhere to go. It felt like my family, that I was not alone.

We hope to share with you, the reader, that this is about the teachers, the new ones and the veterans, it is about real teachers from whom we can learn great things.

Acknowledgments

Build for your team a feeling of oneness, of dependence on one another, and of strength to be derived by unity.

—Vince Lombardi

This book was made possible by a large team of people and we would like to acknowledge them and their contributions.

To Our Families and Friends: Thank you for your support and gentle push when we needed it. We could not have done this without you. Thank you Andy, Josh, Matt, Annie, Zach, Diana, Kaylee, Anthony, Renato (Gordi), Magda (mom), Carla, Martin, Marty, Carlos, Renato Jr., Lisette, Nicolette, and Monique. A special thank-you to Andy Gudwin, Anthony Wallace, Renato Salazar (Gordi), and Vicky Dobbs for their constant support and assistance.

To Corwin: To the best editor ever, Dan Alpert, thank you for your guidance and gentle support throughout the project. To Megan Bedell, Jane Haenel, and Claire Larson, thank you for keeping us on our toes.

To Florida International University: Your collaboration and vision in working with the school system on this very worthwhile project is very much appreciated. Thank you Dr. Patty Barbetta and Ms. Melanie Morales for your incredible support. Thank you Dr. Ann Nevin for your unstoppable belief in us. You have been our true mentor through it all, always believing in us and mentoring us along the journey.

To the District Office Staff of Miami-Dade County Public Schools: Project GATE was a thriving and powerful project due to your support. A very special thank-you to Mr. Ron Felton, Mr. Will Gordillo, Ms. Rosalia Gallo, Ms. Lourdes Camji, Ms. Ava Byrne, Dr. Christine Master, and Ms. Gloria Kotrady. And a very humble thank-you to Ms. Brucie Ball in her memory, whose belief in us and support to us was always unfailing.

To Magda From Denise: Your heart and soul given to this very special group of teachers was the backbone of its success. You truly gave it your all, and I appreciate you and your sincere caring for the success of each team. Without you, Project GATE would have been just another project.

To the New and Early-Career Teachers and Each One of Their Mentors: We would like to give *you* a heartfelt thank-you for being a part of this project, embracing all that we asked you to handle. Each and every one of you were truly our inspiration. To the mentees, we thank you for your willingness to strive to be the very best you could be, and to the mentors who gave of yourselves unselfishly, we thank you for making a difference in the life of a colleague. Mentees and mentors—you were the meaning of our professional work during the year we were together. You were amazing.

Thank you to the 89 teams, even the ones who wanted to remain nameless!

1. Claudia and Kristin
2. Ingrid and Julie
3. Marisel and Michelle
4. Natalie and Daniel
5. Krisanne and Margaret Joy
6. Leslie and Maria
7. Monica and Deborah
8. Mildred and Marioly
9. Damion and Lillian
10. Mariela and Myleen
11. Pedro and Wendy
12. Flemens and Linda
13. Margie and Kathleen
14. Angel and Mamie
15. Antoinette and Kim
16. Robin and Eileen
17. Maria and Collette
18. Linda and Cynthia
19. Constance and Eileen
20. Karen and David
21. Megan and Jeff
22. Tina and Wendy
23. Cherry and Anita
24. Barbara and Mary
25. Maria and Jan
26. Martiza and Lisa
27. Christina and Monica
28. Maba and Mario
29. Pascale and Deidre
30. Natalie and Barbie
31. Soraya and Jacqueline
32. David and Alina
33. Darcy and Maria
34. Madelin and Daniel
35. Tammy and Aida
36. LaSheika and Lidia
37. Tangela and Damarys
38. Alejandro and Roxanna
39. Martha and Yesenia
40. Alexandra and Debbie
41. Sandra and Raul
42. Rachel and Adrianne
43. Rita and Michelle
44. Maite and Jennifer
45. Ana Maria and Clidia
46. Natasia and Analee
47. Martha and Lilliana
48. Marcus and Maria
49. Yohonn and Liana
50. Jennifer and Dona

51. Star and Kelly
52. Carmen and Yvette
53. Rafael and Dayana
54. Smith and Lisa
55. Jaimy and Lourdes
56. Elizabeth and Andriane
57. Olivia and Michelle
58. Ayasha and Myra
59. Maria and Tania
60. Carin and Martha
61. Clemistine and Viviana
62. Jessica and Diane
63. Karol and Olivia
64. Michelle and Rosa
65. Rocia and Selma
66. Irlande and Steven
67. Patrick and Carlos
68. Carmen and Martha
69. Felipe and Lora
70. Janeth and Maria
71. Natasha and Marlen
72. Doris and Janet
73. Katrisha and John
74. Jacqueline and Myra
75. Anthony and Tan
76. Lynette and Sonya
77. Giomar and Iliana
78. Cristina and Evelys
79. Iliana and Peter
80. Lourdes and Maria
81. Tamara and Renett
82. Kaljanca and Joanne

To Joanna and Jocelyn: Thank you for sharing your words of wisdom with us.

PUBLISHER'S ACKNOWLEDGMENTS

Corwin would like to acknowledge the contributions of the following individuals:

Rosemary Burnett, District Mentor Consultant
School District of La Crosse
La Crosse, WI

Victoria Duff, Mentor Training Coordinator
New Jersey Department of Education, Office of Professional Standards
Trenton, NJ

Belinda Gimbert, Staff Developer
Newport News Public Schools
Newport News, VA

Mike Greenwood, District Teacher Leader
Windsor Public Schools
Windsor, CT

Deborah Howard, Curriculum Coordinator
Governor Baxter School for the Deaf
Falmouth, ME

Deborah Long, BTSA Induction Coordinator
Merced Union High School District
Merced, CA

Mindy Meyer, Project Director
New Teacher Alliance, Center for Strengthening the Teaching Profession
Tacoma, WA

About the Authors

 **Denise M. Gudwin, PhD,** is currently an adjunct professor at Florida International University and consultant for the Bureau of Education and Research. Before her retirement from Miami-Dade County Public Schools after thirty years, her past experiences in the fourth largest school district included (1) teacher; (2) district curriculum support specialist; (3) district instructional supervisor, programs for learning disabilities; and (4) district executive director, Office of Professional Development and Center for Professional Learning. Dr. Gudwin's graduate work includes a master's degree in reading and a PhD in education leadership with a focus on teaching reading to students with learning disabilities. Her areas of interests are literacy, learning disabilities, teacher support, and research.

She is past president of Council for Exceptional Children, Miami Chapter, and has been on the state board for Florida Council for Exceptional Children, and Florida Division of Learning Disabilities.

Dr. Gudwin's publications include numerous teacher manuals on effective literacy strategies and response to intervention with the Bureau of Education and Research and success of preservice teachers in an ERIC document, as well as co-authoring articles on teacher retention, professional development, and early literacy in *Journal of Urban Learning, Teaching, and Research*, *Florida Educational Leadership Journal*, and the Wright Group/McGraw-Hill Early Wright Skills Program. Dr. Gudwin has also contributed as a peer reviewer for *Reading Teacher Journal* (Volumes 56 and 57).

Dr. Gudwin has presented seminars on effective literacy strategies, response to intervention, co-teaching, inclusion, differentiated instruction, and learning disabilities in over twenty-five states and Canada.

Conferences at which her papers have been presented include American Educational Research Association, International Reading Association, Florida Reading Association, Florida Council for Exceptional Children, Florida Inclusion Network Conference; Eastern Educational Research Association; Norma Bossard Literacy Conference; Celebration of the Young Child Seminar; and Division for Learning Disabilities Florida Conference. Honors awarded to Dr. Gudwin include Florida's Landis Stetler Award (Council for Exceptional Children); Reading Professor of the Year Award (Dade Reading Council, Affiliate of the Florida Reading

Association and International Reading Association); Bernice O. Johnson LD Award (State Division of Learning Disabilities CEC); "Ideals of the PTA" for Dade County; "Teacher of the Year" Award, Dr. Gilbert L. Porter Elementary School and Pine Lake Elementary; and Impact Grant recipient from Dade Public Education Fund. Dr. Gudwin has had numerous guest appearances on the public radio and television programs *B.O.L.D. Presents, You Should Know,* and *Misunderstood Minds.*

 **Magda D. Salazar-Wallace** is currently the special education chairperson and teacher at an elementary school in the fourth largest school district of the nation. Her past experiences include (1) inclusion teacher, (2) curriculum support specialist, (3) professional development support specialist, and (4) adjunct professor at Florida International University and Barry University. She is a former Rookie Teacher of the Year.

Mrs. Salazar-Wallace's graduate achievements include a master's degree in reading. She is a doctoral candidate in education in the Urbana S.E.A.L.S. project at Florida International University, Miami's first Research I Public University. Her areas of interests are new and early-career teachers, special education, legislation and compliance in special education, learning disabilities, and over-representation of minorities in special education, literacy, and research.

Mrs. Salazar-Wallace's past responsibilities include vice-president, Council for Exceptional Children (CEC), Miami Chapter 121; newsletter editor, Florida Council for Exceptional Children (FCEC); and local program chair, 2007 State FCEC Conference. Mrs. Salazar-Wallace's publications include ERIC documents and co-authored articles in *Journal of Urban Learning, Teaching, and Research, Florida Educational Leadership Journal,* as well as in the *National Journal of Urban Education and Practice.* She has contributed articles to *Dade Dispatch* (the Quarterly Newsletter for Dade Reading Council) and to *ESE Connection* (newsletter for the Florida Council for Exceptional Children), in which she authored a column titled, "Multicultural Corner." In addition, she was co-editor of the *GATE Gazette* (a monthly newsletter for beginning teachers and their mentors).

Mrs. Salazar-Wallace's presentations include the following professional development sessions for Miami-Dade County Public Schools: *Best Practices in Teaching Reading; Early Literacy for K–2 Teachers of Students With Disabilities; Reading and Writing Standards for Elementary and Secondary Teachers; Accommodations and Interdisciplinary Strategies and Practices for the SPED Teacher;* and *How Do I Include ALL Diverse Learners AND Increase Achievement.*

Mrs. Salazar-Wallace has presented at the National Conference of the Council for Exceptional Children, the Florida Council for Exceptional Children, Norma Bossard Literary Conference, Dade Reading Council, 9th Annual Celebration of the Young Child Seminar, Florida Reading Association Conference, the Florida Federation Council for Exceptional Children Conference, and the Florida Kindergarten Council. Presently, she has submitted presentations on coaching and mentoring that are under review. Additionally, she was a guest on a television show discussing first-year teachers.

People come into your life for a reason, a season, or a lifetime.

*When someone is in your life for a **REASON**, it is usually to meet a need you have expressed. They have come to assist you through a difficulty, to provide you with guidance and support, to aid you physically, emotionally, or spiritually. They may seem like a godsend, and they are! They are there for the reason you need them to be. Then, without any wrongdoing on your part, or at an inconvenient time, this person will say or do something to bring the relationship to an end. Sometimes they die. Sometimes they walk away.*

Sometimes they act up and force you to take a stand.

What we must realize is that our need has been met, our desire fulfilled, their work is done.

And now it is time to move on.

*Then people come into your life for a **SEASON**, because your turn has come to share, grow, or learn. They bring you an experience of peace, or make you laugh. They may teach you something you have never done. They usually give you an unbelievable amount of joy. Believe it! It is real! But, only for a season.*

LIFETIME *relationships teach you lifetime lessons: things you must build upon in order to have a solid emotional foundation. Your job is to accept the lesson, love the person, and put what you have learned to use in all other relationships and areas of your life. It is said that love is blind but friendship is clairvoyant.*

—Author Unknown

As we continue to make a difference in teachers' lives through our experiences with mentoring relationships, both mentors and mentees may come into our lives for a reason, a season, or a lifetime.

We, the authors, are fortunate that our two paths have crossed for a lifetime.

—Denise and Magda

Teacher-to-Teacher

Making a Difference

A master can tell you what he expects of you. A teacher, though, awakens your own expectations.

—Patricia Neal

As you read Chapter 1, we encourage you to reflect upon the following thoughts and questions:

1. Reflect on a current mentoring relationship you have or would like to have.

2. What are the key components of an effective teacher-to-teacher relationship? What works and what does not work?

3. Mentors are . . .

To help you discover your own understandings of these questions, the content of the chapter is organized in the following sections: Teachers Making a Difference, Enhanced Personal Growth, Mentoring, From the Voice of Magda, and From the Voice of Denise. We anchor the content in the context of various scenarios that illustrate the concept of teachers making a difference.

TEACHERS MAKING A DIFFERENCE

Teachers can and do make a difference in each other's lives. Veteran teachers who serve as mentors are known to be influential in the retention of new teachers (Billingsley, 2005). Many of us have been there—most of us have been new teachers, some of us have been mentors. We have seen firsthand the difference that one individual can make in our lives. At the core of national reform is the role of the teacher (Kliebard, 2004). The teacher's role in this sometimes-challenging profession is absolutely and without a doubt one of the most important roles in the school. Think of all the people you know in all different walks of life, people of diverse cultural backgrounds, people of varied intelligence and experience, short ones, tall ones, young ones, older ones—each and every individual has been influenced by a teacher. What can be done to ensure that the role of the teacher is of utmost priority to a school system? According to Stansbury and Zimmerman (2002), "A third of beginning teachers quit within their first three years on the job. We don't stand for this kind of dropout rate among students, and we can no longer afford it in our teaching ranks" (p. 10). Comparing the retention of our teachers with student retention is a new twist—Stansbury and Zimmerman make a strong point: We don't tolerate that among students, and we should not tolerate it in our profession. In general, we have found that mentoring programs are critical for the success of new teachers, and a focused program dealing with specific issues such as special education can be beneficial (Salazar, Gudwin, & Nevin, 2008).

ENHANCED PERSONAL GROWTH

Brock and Grady (2007) suggest that such programs expect multiple outcomes, such as retention of qualified teachers and enhanced professional growth. How can teacher leaders help new and early-career teachers thrive in many diverse settings, including a challenging multicultural school district, where there may be over 100 different cultures? In our diverse classrooms, we must be equipped with skills of quality teaching, a positive attitude, a love of learning more about ourselves and others, and the ability to reach a diverse group of teachers and students where there are sometimes more cultures represented in one school than we ever thought possible, at times when we are asked to deal with **intercultural** issues that we may not even be aware of—these important issues are interwoven into the fabric of this book.

It is our goal to enhance your professional growth and demonstrate the guiding factors in the successful teaching experiences.

Such enhanced professional growth is demonstrated in the aspect of mentoring, in which we, the authors, have been involved between us for a combined total of eighteen years. In fact, we ourselves represent the positive outcomes of mentoring: We have worked together for nine years, beginning in the capacity of university professor and undergraduate student, moving into professor and graduate student, from support personnel to new teachers, to supervisor, to colleagues at the central office level and presently as co-authors, with a passion for the field of education. Both of us have alternately taken the lead in the role of mentor in this partnership, with personal and professional growth as an ongoing outcome.

MENTORING

Mentor (noun): lifelong learner, supporter, friend, guide, listener, and role model

Mentor (verb): to observe, listen, analyze, discuss, guide, support

The term *mentor* originated in Greek mythology, initially coming from "Homer's *Odyssey*, in which a wise and learned man called Mentor was given the task of educating Odysseus' son" (Pitton, 2000, p. 13), to guide him on the journey to maturity, nurturing him, serving as a trusted friend, and providing a model for what we now refer to as mentoring (Brock & Grady, 2007). What is a mentor? Mentors facilitate learning, model and demonstrate lessons, co-plan, co-teach, and provide feedback, while building and maintaining a trusting relationship (Killion & Harrison, 2005). When tied together with instructional coaching, mentors can help new and early-career teachers see their teaching world through a different lens (McNeil & Klink, 2004).

High-quality mentoring partnerships provide the new and early-career teacher with an opportunity to work closely with and learn from an experienced teacher. The partnership is fostered by structured collegial exchanges, such as peer observations, face-to-face conversations outside of school hours, and effective communication via e-mail or telephone, in which the new and early-career teacher and mentor participate together. Structured time is set aside as a necessary part of the collaborative collegial exchange, as it enables collaborating activities such as co-planning, co-teaching, modeling, and reflecting to take place.

> Most importantly, a great camaraderie is formed, where students ultimately benefit from quality instruction.
>
> —Liana, mentor

When mentors deal with new and early-career teachers who are different in the sense of ethnicity, culture, linguistics, or age, some considerations need to be taken to avoid making judgments. We want to always be sensitive to the differences in the following:

- Time management
  - Time doesn't always mean the same to all people. Some people feel strongly that socialization is a major part of getting things done. For example, some teachers in the black, non-Hispanic and Hispanic communities weigh heavily on the social connections, which may impact their timeframes. Additionally, in some communities, it is not uncommon to schedule an event an hour before it is really supposed to start, just so that everyone will be "on time" for that event. There are subtle cultural differences to which we must be sensitive without making judgments.

- Levels of excitability
  - Some cultures are known for their passion and excitement, such as people from Italian and certain Hispanic heritages. It is the makeup of their personality. As we become more sensitive to our differences, we will understand them more easily.
- Tone of voice or loudness of voice
  - Some cultures, such as Asian and some Central and South Americans, are known to have a soft, quieter tone of voice, while those from Cuba and Puerto Rico, Italy, and some other European countries may be known for a louder, firmer-type tone of voice. These same variances are even seen in different regions of the United States. It doesn't always portray shyness or assertiveness; it is just the culture of the language and the ways of the people that often come across in communication.
- Age
  - People of various age groups may respond in ways that are common for their age group. For example, an older teacher may respond in a way that is normal for her, yet very strange to a much younger teacher. We personally know older teachers who do not know the first thing about text messaging on a cell phone and have no desire to change that, yet in working with a younger teacher, sending a brief text message, "How are things going today?" might be just the pick-me-up that a younger teacher needs. However, we must embrace our differences and not make judgments about them.
- Values
  - The value systems of various cultural groups have a spectrum of what is consistent with their culture. For example, extended families might be extremely important to a Central American teacher, where many members of the family live together, yet that concept may be quite unusual for a teacher from another cultural group.
- Personality types
  - A variation of personality types exists over all groups of people, not dependent on culture, linguistics, or age; sensitivity to what makes each of us the way we are will be beneficial to any mentoring relationship.

In striving for an effective teacher-to-teacher mentoring relationship, we need to keep those differences in mind and be sensitive to the basic differences in all people—especially those teachers we mentor. This is the diversity that makes for a wonderful world in which we live.

As an example in looking at differences in people, Magda started out as an undergraduate student in her twenties from a Central American background, mentored by Denise, an older white forty-something woman. We would like to share our take on this whole mentoring concept from our own personal points of view.

FROM THE VOICE OF MAGDA

In recollection, how we arrived at this process is still unknown to me. So I will retell from what I recall now, which is sketchy since I am in the process of planning for my wedding, writing my dissertation, and co-authoring this book, while trying to still have a social life. In 1999, I enrolled at Barry University as a student in hopes of achieving my bachelor of education degree. I worked at ARC Project Thrive, a private school for preschool students with disabilities. I left fifteen minutes early from work each day to arrive at school on time, and I was in school five days a week for roughly three hours a day. I was in an accelerated program. I am a very organized person and put forth more than usual effort. My first semester was somewhat of an adjustment period. I was going from a part-time to a full-time student and working on my major. This is the time when I met Denise. She was working for the central office, working on her dissertation, as well as adjuncting for two local universities. Talk about having a full plate . . . or platter, I should say. Yet she had the time to provide feedback and communicate with all of her students and provide e-mail or phone communication in regard to the coursework, and even on private matters. I clearly remember one Thanksgiving holiday. Denise was visiting her family in Seattle, and I needed help with a class assignment for her course. She provided a detailed clarification of the assignment requirements, a conversation that lasted well over twenty minutes. I believe this is where the journey of our mentoring relationship began. She aided in helping me become a stellar student—it was her high expectations that I strived to meet and her words of encouragement and confidence that eventually led to my drive for my scholarly endeavors. After a couple of years, our relationship from student to professor evolved to one of beginning teacher to central office relationship. As a first-year teacher, I put into practice all that I had learned while at the university. I created books as she taught us; I got involved at the school level; and, as she highly encouraged me to do, I began my master's program. During my first year, I also joined a support group for beginning teachers, which met after school in Mrs. Gudwin's work site. There, a group of beginning teachers networked and discussed challenges we were facing. She was instrumental in making my first year a success. During the next couple of years, we communicated and occasionally met for dinner as we worked together on several projects. She visited my classroom periodically and presented parent workshops at my school, as well as teacher professional development sessions. Our relationship eventually shaped into one of a more collegial relationship when I came to work for her at the central office. I had acquired enough experience, content knowledge, and confidence in myself that I finally no longer referred to her as Professor Gudwin or Dr. Gudwin, but rather Denise. This truly was reflective of what our relationship had grown into: a reciprocal relationship where I had been coached and was now capable of coaching her if need be. Coaching comes in many forms, and our relationship involved coaching in a nonjudgmental manner that led us to a journey where we were comfortable with each other, accepting of each other, and maintained an open communication. I hope to think that we have given to each other quite equally in various roles.

FROM THE VOICE OF DENISE

From my perspective, as a mentor early on in the relationship with Magda, I didn't even realize I *was* a "mentor." My goal was to be a really good university professor, provide all that I could to my students, and share with them the love of teaching and learning. In the process, I became a mentor to Magda. Exactly when did that happen? I'm not even sure! Was it purposeful? It definitely became purposeful, but it may not have been at the very beginning stages of our relationship. Part of the joy of a mentoring relationship is that the mentor learns as much from the mentee as the mentee learns from the mentor. It is that reciprocal relationship that I personally continue to embrace, as I learn from Magda with every facet of our continued collaboration. Another part of the joy of the mentoring relationship was the building of a collegial partnership that eventually interwove its way into a friendship, while continuing to nurture both a personal and professional relationship.

Over the past nine years that Magda and I have collaborated on a variety of professional projects, we have done so in the following capacities in the workplace:

Mentor: Denise	Mentee: Magda
University professor	Undergraduate student
University club sponsor	President of student organization
District support personnel	New teacher
University professor	Graduate student
District administrator	Employee, curriculum support specialist
District administrator	Employee, professional development specialist
Colleague	Colleague

Additionally, beyond the workplace, we have evolved into additional mentoring relationships of best friends, sisters, and even at rare times, mother/daughter, with each of us taking the role of the mentor from time to time, sharing the leadership role, balancing the role while interchanging places as needed or desired. We even co-chaired a state conference together for a state affiliate of the Council for Exceptional Children (CEC), which involved a year of planning, organizing, coordinating, and implementing. We decided if our relationship could withstand that journey, we could survive anything!

Back in the beginning of our mentoring relationship, and probably the glue that adhered our solid bond, I have vivid pictures of communication— a critical component that, if missing, erases the possibility of mentoring even taking place. One such communication occurred when I was on vacation during the Thanksgiving holiday while I was the university professor of an undergraduate course, of which Magda was a student. I was sitting cross-legged in a soft-pillowed wicker rocking chair by a sunny window at my brother's house with my laptop on my lap, answering e-mails from Magda, writing back on an instant message, reviewing a paper of hers from another class for which she had asked me for grammatical assistance, all the while my family asking me sarcastically, "Why is it so important that you work while we are on vacation?" But I didn't view it as work—I was just helping her out on something, or answering a question, or chatting about her family. She had the extraordinary ability to consistently communicate with her professors (still does to this day), pulling me into her world, truly initiating the mentoring relationship. Over the years, we have successfully lived the mentoring relationship and have both become stronger professionals because of it.

Morris Zelditch's (1990) description of mentors continually shows up in numerous references (Institute Student Mentor Programme, 2007; Johnston, 2008; University of Michigan, 2006). To paraphrase Zelditch:

Mentors are advisors, people with career experience willing to share their knowledge.

Mentors are supporters, people who give emotional and moral encouragement.

Mentors are tutors, people who give specific feedback on one's performance.

Mentors are masters, in the sense of employers to whom one is apprenticed.

Mentors are sponsors, sources of information and aids in obtaining opportunities.

Mentors are models, of identity, of the kind of person one should be, to be an academic.

There are times that I am the mentor, the advisor, and there are times that Magda holds that torch. There have been times both professionally and personally that I am the mentor, the supporter, and there are times that Magda takes on that role. There are times when we both become the master, the sponsor, and the model, showing that mentorship is a fluid concept that grows and changes as we ourselves continue to grow and change.

Mentoring words that come to mind when I think of Magda's and my strong mentoring partnership: *safe, nonjudgmental, harmony, teaching, potential, direction, communication, encouragement, journey, comfort, acceptance, guiding.* If reading this book guides other individuals to form quality mentoring partnerships, then a good deed has been completed. Mentoring is, as our experiences demonstrate to all, a goal for which to strive and an opportunity that will enrich both the personal and professional lives of the mentor and mentee. It is a teacher-to-teacher relationship, making a difference.

One Saturday morning, sharing breakfast out at a local restaurant with my husband, I overheard a conversation at the table next to me where an obviously experienced athletic coach wearing the hat of a mentor for three young players shared two bits of wisdom with them. "If I'm not ready for anything and everything, I am not a good coach," he said to his young players. I expanded this personally in many directions (a text-to-self strategy, for those of you who are reading teachers!), two of which were (1) a teacher working with a struggling student needs to be ready for anything and everything, and (2) a mentor working with a mentee should be ready for whatever needs are to be met. As mentors and instructional coaches, we too have to be ready for anything and everything. Sometimes we are the only lifelines our mentees have. The other words of wisdom this coach imparted to his mentees over breakfast: "You should be tired after that practice. Or you didn't give it your all. That's what it takes." Just a matter-of-fact statement voiced with conviction while he ate his fried eggs and grits. But what an impact it had on me. Yes, sometimes we get tired in both our roles of mentors and mentees, as we should. We do need to give it our all, because in the words of that obviously experienced coach and mentor, "That's what it takes."

The Voice of the Struggling Teacher

Teaching is more than imparting knowledge, it is inspiring change.
Learning is more than absorbing facts, it is acquiring understanding.

—William Arthur Ward

As you read Chapter 2, we encourage you to reflect upon the following questions:

1. What can we learn from listening to the voices of struggling new teachers?

2. What are the struggles new teachers face?

3. What can we do to anticipate and provide appropriate and nurturing assistance before they truly need it?

To help you discover your own understandings of these questions, the content of the chapter is organized in the following sections: Typical Stages of Teacher Development, Struggles, Joys, and Managing Tips. We anchor the content in the context of various scenarios that illustrate the voice of the struggling teacher.

Spotlight on Pierre

Let's look at Pierre's classroom. On his fourth day on the job, as a brand-new teacher, he was faced with challenges head-on that neither he nor his mentor, a highly qualified, National Board Certified Teacher who loves his profession, had any idea how to deal with or "fix" for that matter. After day four of the career he thought was his calling, Pierre is ready to throw in the towel. With his bachelor's and master's degrees in hand, he is ready to quit. Put yourself in Pierre's shoes: Have you ever felt that kind of frustration before? Have you ever wanted to quit?

Martin Luther King Senior High School is in the heart of a poverty-stricken, metropolitan area, a hard-to-staff school, with 80% of the students living in the public housing neighborhood. The ninth- through twelfth-grade school has a 61% free and reduced lunch rate, with a student population of 1% white, non-Hispanic; 94% black, non-Hispanic; and 5% Hispanic; and a teacher population of 22% white, non-Hispanic; 52% black, non-Hispanic; 17% Hispanic; and 9% Asian or Native American.

Let's read about Pierre's fourth day on the job:

Things happened today that I really don't feel prepared to handle. It's my fourth day teaching. Yesterday there was central office staff at our school, trying to assist our total school, which is viewed as low performing, and recommending that I rearrange my classroom to make it a more conducive learning environment. It honestly feels like they are all attacking us, but I know they are trying to help. Today, and remember, this is my fourth day, I was scheduled to have a meeting with a group of professionals, including a student advocate and an attorney. That was stressful beyond belief. But it didn't even take place because of what happened thirty minutes before the meeting when the central office staff again observed my classroom. They were nicely dressed, important-looking people. The students were pretty good at first. I was a little nervous with all of them in my room. And then, it all fell apart. There is a special education student placed in my classroom who has some special problems. I don't know if I'm equipped to handle him. I really didn't learn some of these things in college. On his way to the bathroom, he began pulling his pants down. We tried to get him to the bathroom in time because he has this problem, but as he was walking with us to the bathroom, he accidentally hit R. [a student] in the back of the head. R. thought it was Ms. T [another teacher], and he knocked over a desk and hauled himself toward the teacher, knocking her down to the ground, while she toppled into a central office lady, knocking her to the ground as well. R. then began hitting Ms. T all over the place. She started bleeding. Someone pushed the emergency call button and the office staff said in a totally sarcastic tone, "What is it this time?" We needed her to call 911. Ms. T. was bleeding and managed to stand up, only to faint and fall to the floor again. It took five adults to hold down R. I haven't been trained in how to deal with this type of student. And I'm not sure I want to . . . I didn't go to college for this . . . What can I do? I just want to quit, but I went to school to become a teacher.

There are other "Pierres" out there who need guidance and support for them to remain committed to this new profession on which they are embarking. There are many mentoring programs across the nation, but to be there as a lifeline for Pierre, we have to be in a trusted support relationship that is nonjudgmental. Pierre wanted to be successful but was hit fist-to-face with immediate challenges and obstacles. What if Pierre had not had a mentor? Would the school staff have known of his struggles? If you were the mentor, what suggestions might you provide to pick Pierre up and give him concrete assistance? If you were Pierre, and did not have a mentor, what would you have done next?

According to the *New Orleans CityBusiness* BNet poll (2005), out of 1,065 survey respondents, 6.2% of teenagers from ages 13 through 18 wanted to be teachers when they grew up. The exact same percent of respondents surveyed on the same poll (6.2%) stated that they wanted to be doctors. One of the most popular reasons to be a teacher is the idea of helping children, to make a difference in a child's or young adult's world. New teachers who grew up wanting to be teachers probably never thought of the day-to-day struggles they now face. We don't anticipate overcoming difficulties and continuing to struggle; we anticipate overcoming the difficulties.

Many school districts are currently faced with critical shortages of teachers and other education professions; the supply-and-demand gap widens for areas such as special education in urban settings. Struggling students and struggling schools need assistance, and it is the same for struggling teachers. We will include a discussion of the stages of development (anticipation, survival, disillusionment, rejuvenation, reflection, and anticipation) that new teachers face and the implications of the support provided. We will continue this dialogue or conversation and will take this a step further in the next chapter, where we will listen to the voices of the teachers; these voices are often missing from the planning stages of induction programs. They will continue to provide insight on the core feelings and frustrations, the emotional ups and downs of which induction program developers, as well as teacher leader mentors, need to be aware.

As we listen to their voices, the perspectives of new and early-career teachers and the struggles and joys of the day-to-day personal and professional experiences they encounter in a multicultural setting can give us insight on what they need, if we listen. They know their goals and where they are heading, and they know when they are faltering. "Retention of beginning teachers and prevention of burnout continue to challenge school personnel" (Salazar, Gudwin, & Nevin, 2008, p. 50). We must nurture that role of the teacher, not let it be torn down.

TYPICAL STAGES OF TEACHER DEVELOPMENT

Ellen Moir (1999) discusses the challenges that new teachers face and the support that new teachers need. She looks at these early teaching experiences as five, sometimes six distinct phases. We have added actual e-mails that coincide with each of the phases, in the hope of helping you visualize the stages of teacher development through the eyes of Grace, a first-year teacher:

1. **Anticipation Phase:** This begins before the new teacher even enters the field of teaching. It is that awesome feeling of excitement and anticipation that the beginning teacher feels. It is the "I can do anything; I can't wait to begin teaching" feeling. This phase typically starts during the preservice undergraduate time, and lasts through the first few weeks of teaching. It is a wonderful beginning phase that keeps us floating, while eagerly looking forward to our new profession.

Dear Christy,

It was a pleasure meeting you at the kickoff for new teachers. I must say, this summer, when I first got hired, I was a little overwhelmed with finishing school and moving into a new apartment. But, now, I cannot wait to set up my classroom. I am so excited. All the great ideas that I learned at the university will be put to good use! I will set up a cooperative learning environment where all students will be successful—every one of them will learn.

In less than two weeks, school will start and I will have a classroom all to myself! I have not yet seen my room, but I will after the staff development I must attend. I will let you know how that goes.

Thanks again for being my mentor. I cannot wait to have you come make a collegial visit.

Ms. Grace Cain
First-Grade Teacher
Ransom Elementary

❖ ❖ ❖ ❖ ❖

Dear Christy,

Thank you for the cute e-mail you sent me. I will think of it as I meet my students. As you know, tomorrow is the first day of school and I cannot wait! I want to meet my little ones. I set up my centers and the place for my rules, which we will write together. I have also contacted all my students' parents and welcomed them to my classroom. I gave them my telephone and e-mail and invited them to come by any time during my planning. I cannot wait. I doubt I'll sleep tonight, but I know I must. Oh my . . . I cannot wait.

Ms. Grace Cain
First-Grade Teacher
Ransom Elementary

❖ ❖ ❖ ❖ ❖

Dear Christy,

It was a wonderful first week. I'm so energized with my students who were just the cutest! I haven't introduced my rules yet, nor did I get them to rotate centers, but we did do a great activity for back to school. We familiarized ourselves with the school and our schedule. I'm just a little concerned about having a couple of students who do not speak English. I thought they were in a separate class? Anyway, I love teaching!

Ms. Grace Cain
First-Grade Teacher
Ransom Elementary

2. **Survival Phase:** The rapid pace of all that the new teacher has to learn and deal with and overwhelming feelings associated with the beginning of the school year often keep new teachers struggling just to keep their heads above water. This phase often includes bargaining feelings of, "If I can just get through the morning..." "If I can get through until lunchtime..." "If I can just make it to dismissal time..." The workload and emotions that come spiraling toward the new teacher are so overpowering that oftentimes just getting through the next minute, the next hour, or the rest of the day is the primary goal. How do I complete my lesson plans? Who do I ask for help in setting up my grade book? What do I do with the thirteen students who are out of control? When do I give up? Where do I get ideas for teaching? Tons of questions are hitting the new teacher at a quick pace.

Five or six e-mails are exchanged over the next couple of weeks. In October, Grace sends the following e-mail:

Dear Christy,

I am sorry that I have not responded to your e-mail in over a week. I know you are supposed to come and provide a collegial exchange, but I am so overwhelmed. I just try to get through each day. I have a student that runs out of my classroom.

Remember the kids who didn't speak English? Well, I am still having a hard time using appropriate strategies.

I try to settle my kids down after lunch so I can teach math and as soon as I do, as soon as they get settled, we have to go to music. As organized as I am, my papers are all over the classroom. The centers are nicely set up, but we haven't been able to use them. I am at work from sunrise to sunset and I think I've managed to lose about seven pounds. Can we meet next week? I still have about two loads of grading to do and I am just too exhausted.

3. **Disillusionment Phase:** The realization that it is not getting any better finally hits. There are stressful situations coming at new teachers fast and furiously even after two months on the job. This is the time that some teachers break down and cry, as they struggle with their self-confidence, wondering why they chose this profession. Is this what they really thought they wanted to do? "It is not working out the way I thought it would. What should I do now?" In addition to the already stressful first few months, the new situations to handle may even include challenging parents at a schoolwide open house and ongoing communication with other teachers, as well as a possible observation from the school administration. Some new teachers find themselves ready to throw in the towel.

Dear Christy,

I was glad we just had an extra day to recover. I slept most of Sunday and Monday. And I see in our calendar that we do not have any more days until December. I don't think I can do it. I have not been able to do lesson plans for math for two weeks and my reading/language arts groups are such a challenge. I just keep teaching through the teacher manuals without any thought. My paperwork is late to administration the majority of the time. Luckily, they know I am new so they have some sort of understanding and sympathy. I have tried six different types of classroom management and nothing seems to work. I have four students with disabilities, three that cannot identify even two letters, and four that do not speak English. I am not sure that this is for me.

In December, Grace sends the following e-mail:

Dear Christy,

Teaching is not supposed to be this way. All the things I learned in college couldn't prepare me for this. I thought I'd be able to set up my classroom management and actually have it work. By now, I figured my kids could rotate independently to the centers, so that I can work with my low readers in guided reading. I am constantly redirecting the students to listen and follow directions. I have parents calling me all the time. I don't know that I can make it to the end of the school year, let alone through winter recess. I cannot wait until the two weeks of VACATION! But I cannot even go on vacation because I've spent so much on supplies for my classroom that I have no money and still need some things for my classroom, and I'll probably still be catching up on my grading.

4. **Rejuvenation Phase:** Typically in January, new teachers have a better understanding of the system and process, and become more excited at being able to achieve their goals. They may have had a restful yet fun two-week winter break and have had time to pull it together again. The second semester may bring new feelings of "I can do this!" Excitement and motivation set in, and a sense of renewal surrounds their newfound energy.

In January, Grace sends Christy the following e-mail:

Dear Christy,

A Happy New Year to you . . . and a Happy New Year to me! I took a couple of days to relax and be at home with family, but then I went to the teacher store down the block and bought some things. I reread some of my books from school and I know I can do this! I'm ready.

5. **Reflection Phase:** The end is in sight, and the anticipation of being an even better teacher next year builds. This phase often occurs in late spring, and dreams of their future classrooms and students keep them going.

Dear Christy,

Spring break just passed. It gave me an opportunity to reflect upon this past year. As it was stated in the newsletter for new teachers, "At the heart of every effective teacher is the reflective teacher." I was able to reflect about learning and effective teaching. I reflected upon what I saw in your classroom, what I saw in mine. Thank you for the opportunity to do that.

As reflection moves stronger into anticipation, first-year teachers feel they can truly make a career out of this wonderful profession.

Dear Christy,

Summer break is upon us and I cannot wait. You probably think I cannot wait to go on vacation, but in reality, I cannot wait to get back to my second year of teaching. What I've been doing for the past couple of days is revisiting the journal that I kept this school year and reflecting upon it, which will allow me to refine my craft, my teaching techniques. I thank you for your help and support because without it, I would have been lost. I cannot wait for next year to roll around. Have a wonderful summer.

Figure 2.1 portrays the new teacher's attitudes during the first school year. Can you relate to each of these stages in some way?

Figure 2.1 Phases of First-Year Teaching: Attitudes Toward Teaching

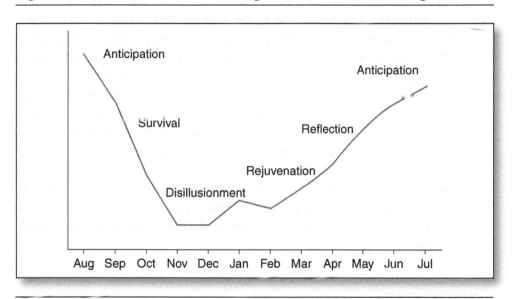

Source: Used by permission from E. Moir, The New Teacher Center, University of California, Santa Cruz.

Along a similar line, although expanded from the first teaching year to multiple years, Harry Wong, author of *How to Be an Effective Teacher: The First Days of School,* during a presentation for new teachers on January 26, 2001, in Miami, Florida, discussed four typical stages a new teacher goes through:

1. **Fantasy:** You feel you know it all. "Teaching" to you means doing fun activities. This is typically the stage from the university to the beginning of a new job in the teaching field.

2. **Survival:** You'll do anything to make it through the next hour. Teaching is a job, it's just a paycheck; busywork is the main thread of the "teaching" going on. [This is the stage where I tell my undergraduate students, "You will cry yourselves home a few times during the first year, asking yourself in between the tears, why you ever thought you wanted to be a teacher." The fact that it is a tough job starts to settle in.]

3. **Mastery:** You start to realize that being a knowledgeable and skillful teacher is the only way to achieve success. Teachers in the mastery stage know how to manage their classroom, teach effectively for mastery, and have high expectations for their students. This stage is often not obtained until three to five years later, after those first few years of fantasy and survival.

4. **Impact:** You know that by using effective teaching practices and knowing how to get your students ready for learning, you are an effective teacher who makes an impact on your students. This stage may not be obvious for years!

It is beneficial for new teachers to know that these stages are common, and that an awareness of them will possibly help in getting through the early stages of their new profession. For teachers who come from diverse backgrounds, be it ethnic, language, or previous experiences, getting through any of the above stages can be even more challenging. One new teacher, Millicent, was surprised to find racial and cultural insensitivity abundant in comments and actions in her new school setting, such as an automatic intolerance of teachers in various ethnic groups, groups of teachers walking and sitting together exclusively. Unfortunately, even in our current times, we are not beyond racial and cultural stereotyping, even in the school setting. Reaching out for support in the form of collegial conversations, mentoring relationships, a peer coach that one can trust, and a friend in the field would be sound recommendations.

What can we do for new teachers as they typically experience these different stages of teacher development? Throughout this book, we continue to weave in numerous strategies and ideas from which to choose, in an effort to provide new teachers and the staff who work with them additional support.

STRUGGLES

Many new teachers come face-to-face with daily challenges that they never expected. Issues such as classroom management, structure, procedures, classroom size, getting along with other teachers, time management, dealing with paperwork, how to utilize support personnel, and many other struggles may open the door to frustration and a roller coaster of emotions, which sometimes lead to the feeling of "I can't do this anymore." Let's look at these issues a little more in depth.

Classroom Management

Classroom management is one of the areas that cause many new teachers to wonder how they are ever going to make it through the school year. A thirty-year-old, second-career beginning teacher shares her struggles with classroom management:

> I feel I should have their respect automatically, I shouldn't have to earn it from them. . . . When I was a kid, I respected my teachers without question. This is not part of my culture. . . . I'm not used to this.

Teaching in culturally diverse urban communities often brings additional challenges with classroom management, which already is seen as a cause of stress in the teaching profession. Classroom management is the one area that more often appears as a hurdle than any other obstacle that the new and early-career teacher must successfully cross. As one third-year teacher shared,

I spend at least 85% of my time with classroom management issues and that leaves only 15% of the time to teach. I think I'm a pretty good teacher and I know how to teach, but I just can't get the students to behave, so I end up spending very little time teaching. I don't know what to do; most of my colleagues just accept the fact and lower their expectations. I don't want to do that.

Just what is classroom management? How do we define something that new and seasoned teachers alike find so difficult? Davis (2007) shares effective classroom discipline as rights and responsibilities, such as the right to be safe and to learn, and the responsibility to be polite and use time wisely. Wong and Wong (1998) share classroom management as procedures to be consistently followed. Bos and Vaughn (2002) look at individual student behavior and the support that individual students may need, which reduces problem behaviors and helps develop appropriate behaviors. According to Friend and Bursuck (2006), "Teachers who communicate respect and trust to their students are more successful in creating positive classroom environments in which fewer behavior problems occur" (p. 159). In agreement is Catherine McTamaney (ninth- through twelfth-grade teacher in Tennessee), "Always live up to the same rules you set up for them. Keep them simple and justifiable. Respect is the only rule I have on my classroom wall" (DePaul, 1998, p. 9).

I don't like to have too many rules or kids will forget them. My students help set up the rules, which makes them more respectful of them.

—Mark White, fifth grade, Nebraska (DePaul, 1998, p. 9)

Some see classroom management as going beyond merely rules and also focusing on setting up procedures. According to Harry Wong (2001), procedures plus routines equal structure. "The number one problem in the classroom is not discipline; it is the lack of procedures and routine. . . . Show me a teacher that says, 'How many times do I have to tell you?' and I will show you who is the slow learner."

Stephanie, a first-year teacher unsure of herself, was assigned Lissette, a very procedures-based seasoned teacher, as a peer teacher. Lissette knew that the time and energy spent setting up the procedures in her classroom paid off on a daily basis. There were consistent procedures in place on everything: what to do as you enter the classroom, when to sharpen pencils, how to set up materials, what to do when your work was finished, what to do when you have a question, where the finished work goes, what to do when the bell rings. Lissette knew that even a first-grade classroom could almost run itself when the procedures were set up and consistently reinforced. That left the majority of the classroom time available for teaching. As she supported Stephanie in her first year, she even rearranged furniture for her, showed her where the materials should be placed, supported her every step of the way. That was a mentoring relationship that truly helped Stephanie's role in her classroom.

Think of a busy metropolitan airport or any of the Walt Disney World theme parks that service thousands of customers every hour. Everyone basically knows what to do; the procedures are in place, from parking to tickets, from which line to stand in to where to get something to eat. The same thing holds true for our classrooms. Once our students know the procedures, effective teaching can more easily take place. Model what you want, explain and show what it looks like, and then practice, practice, practice. Just as an effective athletic coach has plans and procedures for practice, so should a classroom teacher, for optimum outcomes.

Students With Disabilities

The challenge of working with students with disabilities as a beginning general education teacher may bring on even more struggles. As of recently, most college and universities do not mandate special education classes for general education majors. That is starting to change, which is a long time overdue. Florida International University, for example, requires all education majors, no matter the area of focus, to complete a course titled *Teaching Exceptional Students in Inclusive Settings* to prepare all beginning teachers for the diversity that they will experience in their classrooms.

Let's picture that new teacher who just was assigned to a very challenging low-performing diverse school, where many of the students have special needs, although not all of whom are labeled special education. Ms. Garcia's expertise is curriculum—she feels she can handle whatever comes her way in the elementary setting and feels prepared as she begins her first job as a teacher. However, what she isn't ready for are the behavior issues that come flying at her the majority of the day from some of her more challenging students. On Monday, one of the many situations with which she was faced was Christian, who was under the table, yelling he was smarter than his teacher. She didn't know what to do after she had exhausted all of her "tricks" that she thought would work, other than call another teacher over to "take care of him, please." Her main hesitation was not knowing what his disability meant in relation to his inappropriate behavior and not wanting to escalate the situation. She has found she is lacking in knowledge of accommodations and adaptations on how to ensure academic success to those students with disabilities who need more assistance than she knows how to provide. As Ms. Garcia shares,

I just don't know how to reach some of my students. And it is so very frustrating because they take way too much of my time away from my other students. I am not prepared to work with all of these problems. I'm at a loss here.

Having a mentor who can bridge the gap between the general education students and those with special needs would be helpful. Even if the mentor doesn't personally have the specific knowledge, one who knows what and where the resources are at the school site can open doors of information.

Long Hours

Long hours sometimes surprise new teachers and their friends and family. Teaching is so much more than a nine-to-five business job or an eight-hour shift.

> My friends all thought that my job ended at 3 p.m. and that I had the whole summer off, in addition to two weeks in winter and one week at spring break. No one ever told me that I'd be in my classroom past dark, and that I would take work home every day, papers to grade, paperwork to complete, graphs to chart, lesson plans to write, books to read and summarize, lessons to create. . . . Cut and Paste 101, my boyfriend calls it. . . . If I got paid hourly for what I do, I'd be getting minimum wage if I'm lucky.

Teachers work hard, sometimes 50 or more hours a week; about 15% of teachers work 60 hours or more (National Education Association, 2003).

> My professor, Dr. Gudwin, told us to take our vitamins and take care of ourselves because teaching wasn't easy and it would be long hours of work day after day. I didn't realize it until about my second month on the job and the hours weren't getting any better.

Classroom Size

Another area of concern for some new teachers is dealing with classroom size. Sometimes the sheer number of students overwhelms the new and early-career teacher. Annie lamented, "I just stood there with thirty pairs of eyes staring at me on the first day of school and wondered, 'What in the world am I going to do now?'" Conversely, the numbers may be low but the needs high. A class of twelve students, if each has special needs, may at first seem easier, but it is not easy; neither is a class of eighteen English language learners who are at various levels of acquiring their new academic language.

What helps? Organization, procedures in place, and plan, plan, plan! A strategy that I used: The physical space of my classroom was very large, and I didn't feel that I would have enough control with my twenty-eight students, many of whom were known to be quite challenging. I designed the space so that we used half the room at one time, with desk space available for seat work in half the room and floor space available for group work with pillows, beanbags on the floor, and a couch in the other half. That way, the number of students and the physical size of the classroom were used to my advantage instead of the other way around.

For a new teacher who may not think of effective alternatives, a mentor teacher may offer suggestions like the one above.

Getting Along With Co-Workers

Getting along with co-workers can be a challenge in any job. But, as Diane and Jillian found out, when you put two teachers together in one classroom to teach elementary-age students, getting along suddenly becomes a necessary focus. Diane and Jillian are co-teaching in a classroom at a school with a predominately Haitian population. Both teachers are fairly new: Diane is a white, late-twenties new teacher in her second year of teaching who was an education major in college. Jillian is a Haitian young woman who comes from a business background and appreciates order. She began her career as a teaching assistant and is now a first-year teacher. According to Diane,

> Discipline is our biggest difference. I think Jillian thinks I'm too nice. I don't think like her in terms of discipline; I have rules and consequences, but she is more of the disciplinarian than I am. She does it better than I do. She raises her voice; . . . she is stricter. . . . She tells me I smile too much. I don't like to be mean; . . . it makes me feel bad. I don't like that about teaching. We do it in much different ways, but it takes me longer to get the kids settled down because they are not used to my way. . . . It is sometimes a problem. The kids thought I was the helper at the beginning of the year, and I didn't like that.

Just as Marzano (2004) discusses the necessary steps to activate prior knowledge at increasingly deeper levels for our students to achieve, we also must remember the prior knowledge of our colleagues. We may not activate it by using graphic organizers, physical models, or mental images, but we need to be aware of our cultural differences and maintain open dialogues to share our beliefs. As educators, our prior knowledge is what our teaching beliefs are often built upon. Sometimes that means reflecting, biting our tongues and not saying what we are thinking at that time, sitting down and discussing all options—keeping communication open and ongoing in a professional way is a big challenge sometimes. Getting along with our colleagues can be a work in progress, and it is something we have to deal with on a daily basis.

Parent Conferences

Parent conferences can sometimes be quite intimidating to the new and early-career teacher:

> I was so nervous going into the conference. I didn't know what to expect. I hadn't even met the mom yet, and I was so scared that I would mess up. I tried to think ahead of what questions might come up, and I thought I was prepared. But nothing prepared me except actually doing it. Now I feel better, and I know now at least a little of what to expect the next time. It went pretty well, I think. I had to keep my hands in my lap so she wouldn't see me shaking.

I will do a better job the next time. One of my friends told me to make the parents comfortable and to have a plate of cookies for them. I did that, and I think it may have helped. But what helped me most of all is the folder of information I had put together to share with the mom. It opened the conversation on a positive note.

We know of brand-new teachers who had high-profile, intensive parent conferences the first few months of school. Being prepared with student profiles and data helps tremendously in feeling like you know your student. Having your information set up and organized in a binder also works for some teachers.

School Support Staff

Use of paraprofessionals as support personnel may be another learning curve faced by new and early-career teachers. I was a brand-new, first-year, slightly built petite, twenty-two-year-old teacher of white American descent. I walked into my new classroom not knowing what I was going to do first: arrange the piles of tables and chairs that were stacked up in a corner of the room, try to find out who my students were going to be, or try to figure out what materials and supplies I needed and how to get them. I was not even sure what the process was at this school and didn't know whom to ask. I knew one person *not* to ask, because one very grouchy older lady in the office had made it perfectly clear that she was very busy and couldn't be bothered with all those questions, but to put them in writing and leave any communication in her mailbox. I knew I would not ask Mrs. C!

The next day brought a whole new realm of uncertainty when Mrs. Hill walked in my classroom with an air of authority and disdain. Mrs. Hill was a very large, black, non-Hispanic matriarch, both in height and stature, who had been a paraprofessional for twenty years and basically ran the school, or at least acted as if she did. Her reputation and prominence in the largely black, non-Hispanic and Latino community and to the teachers of the migrant school were strong. To top it off, Mrs. Hill was assigned to my new classroom. I honestly felt like the roles should be reversed, that I should be the assistant, and Mrs. Hill should be the teacher. They never covered in college how to handle a paraprofessional or assistant who knows more than you do! New teachers have so much thrown at us during our first week or month on the job that college doesn't prepare us for (and college nowadays includes both education and noneducation majors, which brings a whole new set of "What do I do now?" questions without answers). After the first week of school, the assistant principal came into my classroom and quietly asked me if I had ever worked with support personnel before. Feelings of inadequacy tumbled down on my shoulders. What had Mrs. Hill said to him?

I learned very quickly that collaborative communication worked wonders, as did my own preplanning of what my "assistant" should be doing, a clarification of roles, a schedule of responsibilities, and structure to the classroom setting that focused not only on the students but on the adults in the room as well.

Feeling of Isolation

Many teachers, whether new and early-career or seasoned, at times experience a feeling of isolation, with no one to turn to. Maybe you have felt that too. Sometimes even talented teachers with great potential end up being totally worn out. There have been many comparisons between education, law, medicine, and trades; education has been known as a profession that eats its young, where a "sink-or-swim attitude is apparent" (Gudwin, 2002, p. 46).

In teaching, entry into the profession is sudden. Unlike the business world, where the newcomer goes through a training or apprenticeship period, gradually gaining knowledge, experience, and responsibility, this may not happen in the teaching profession. Newly hired teachers, not just neophyte teachers, are given a key to a room and told to go teach. The trades, such as plumbers and electricians, go into an apprenticeship program, first working as an apprentice, then laboring as a journeyman, and finally qualifying as a licensed tradesman or craftsman. In sports, you begin as a rookie on the bench, slowly gathering knowledge and experience as you work toward a starting position and a higher league (Wong & Wong, as cited in Gudwin, 2002, p. 47). Sometimes the feelings of isolation are so strong that we don't even know whose shoulder to lean on or to whom to turn for help.

Keeping in mind those struggles, let's hear from Jocelyn, an early-career teacher who took a break from the profession after her first year.

Spotlight on Jocelyn

Jocelyn is an early-career teacher who actually quit after her first year but didn't really want to leave the profession. When we visited her classroom in the late spring as a favor to a friend, we found Jocelyn to have great potential as a new teacher. She had the skills she needed, had made an incredible difference with her students as demonstrated by her rapport with them, the increased achievement levels, and the high-stakes test scores; but Jocelyn did not have a mentor and found herself placed in a grade level at the beginning of her first year that was shared with three other brand-new teachers. Along with this situation, plus issues with students with disabilities, classroom management, feelings of isolation, and long hours, she had to quickly learn how to be sensitive to poverty and shootings in the neighborhood. After her first year teaching, she moved across the United States and worked for a year, then returned to her home state and enrolled in a master's degree program. Upon graduation, she returned to the teaching field two years after leaving it. She shares some of her thoughts:

Teaching is so isolating. Some teachers won't even help you; they critique you and talk about you, but won't offer assistance. A teacher can get a bad reputation so fast with one teacher saying, "She can't handle her class," and it carries a lot of weight in the school. It's so sad when that happens. Instead of wanting to help, they talk about them instead. And then the new teacher feels, "I'm a complete loser at this job," and doesn't want to do it anymore. To hear all the talk can be daunting. And sometimes the other teachers just conjure up images about us that aren't even true.

We feel that had she had a mentor and more support, Jocelyn would have stayed in the profession instead of taking a two-year break. We arrived too late during Jocelyn's first year of teaching—and what a shame to have lost a really good first-year teacher. Luckily, we "lost" her for only a short time, and she is back in the classroom making a positive impact on her students.

According to Salazar, Gudwin, and Nevin (2008), beginning teachers often feel isolated; however, communicating with other teachers can "assist in the development of collegiality and collaboration among those who are too often left out of the day-to-day communication and support network" (Boyer & Gillespie, 2003, p. 1.7).

Kardos and Moore Johnson's (2007) study examined experiences of first- and second-year teachers in California, Florida, Massachusetts, and Michigan, and their results revealed that many new teachers report that their "work is solitary, that they are expected to be prematurely expert and independent, and that their fellow teachers do not share a sense of collective responsibility for their school" (Conclusions/Recommendations, ¶ 1). Their day-to-day experiences may be isolated and uninformed. Salazar, Gudwin, and Nevin (2008) point out that the relationships between the presence of collegiality and students' success is strong. A third-year teacher who teaches in a predominately black, non-Hispanic and Latino school sighs,

> Teaching is interesting. You work with your colleagues, but not really *with* them. The kids and you are the real thing. Even though I have a good relationship with some of the teachers, I can't really turn to them for help. I'm expected to do it on my own.

One of the ways to counteract the feeling of isolation is getting involved in the various teams and committees in the school site. It allows new friendships to be formed, encourages the new teacher to become an "expert" sharing a strategy, while earning the respect of colleagues, and facilitates meeting other teachers. One English language learner (ELL) teacher felt very isolated, spending her time with the only other ELL teacher she was assigned to work with, yet found a whole new window of opportunity opening when she joined committees and started collaborating with her peers.

Frustration

While dealing with any and all of the above, frustration may also set in. Jennifer, a white, second-year teacher in a school primarily attended by minority students, describes her feelings of frustration in teaching elementary-age students who don't speak English, many of whom have never been to school before and, at the age of nine, are in a new country with new values and norms, in a classroom for the first time ever. "You have to understand them and what might be going on with them to make it through the day, but it's really hard." Jennifer's other teacher friends from different schools don't understand what she goes through every day. "You don't understand it until you actually do it." As Jennifer shares,

My biggest frustration has been in two areas. One, with classroom management, because I think I'm a good teacher, but I struggle with the discipline. The respect just isn't there. And the second is as a new special education teacher, I know that my kids are in my class because they have difficulties, but it is really frustrating when they just don't get it. I teach it and do a whole dog-and-pony show, and they just don't get it. It sounds terrible and I know they're special ed, and I learned all about it in my master's program, but I did not know just how frustrating it could be until I was actually here, teaching them day after day. I get frustrated with all the DIBELS [Dynamic Indicators of Basic Early Literacy Skills] conversations from the administrative staff—"You have to move them from red to yellow" is all I hear. I don't ever hear *how* to do that. Just that they have to be moved. Over and over and over. They forget that these are kids who have other issues and sometimes learning doesn't come easy for them.

Frustration is also a problem with the cultural differences experienced by our new teachers. Take Teresa's frustration—she was a well-respected teacher in her native county. When she came to the United States, she began as a new teacher again. She was placed in a predominantly white, upper-class school, where she struggled from day one. Teresa has a very heavy Spanish accent, which separated her from the other teachers. Unfortunately, even though she had competent teaching skills, she was looked on as a less-prepared teacher and felt like she continuously had to prove herself. This constantly ate away at her self-esteem and drained her emotionally. After the first semester, she felt teaching was not her thing and started looking for another job outside of the field of education.

Roller Coaster of Emotions

The new teacher is dealing with a roller coaster of emotions during those beginning months, oftentimes without knowing to whom to turn for a listening ear.

At my school, if the teacher doesn't speak Haitian Creole, the parents don't come. They don't know English. We end up having one of the Haitian teachers translate and they do all the talking. Even if they know some English, they usually don't really seem to understand what we're saying. Sometimes our children are the first in the family to even attend a school. When we connect with our students' parents, it is such a feel-good feeling. The respect and caring are evident and we work together. But it just doesn't happen that often. One of my parents just had her ninth child. Sometimes J. has to stay home to help her with the other children. He is in third grade for the third time, and he still can't read. What can I tell the mom at a parent conference? First of all, we have a major language barrier because I don't speak Haitian Creole and she doesn't speak English; second, she is having a difficult time helping him at home; and third, how can I really help? I feel like my hands are tied. We know that the mother's education and the verbal stimulation are so critical to our students, but sometimes I feel like I don't know what else to do. . . . How can I really help him? Sometimes I don't want to call in the parents because I know they will beat [the children], so I end up bargaining with the kids. I won't call some of the parents. . . . I refuse.

In this scenario, it is the language of Haitian Creole, but we can substitute Spanish, Russian, Portuguese, French, Chinese, Japanese, German, or any other language or dialect that represents a variety of cultural groups, as well as various cultural values and mores that affect the family dynamics. Having a trusted someone to turn to might make all the difference in the world, especially if that mentor is sensitive to cultural and linguistic differences.

"I Can't Do This Anymore"

The 2005 National Center for Education Statistics shows that approximately 27.7% of new teachers leave the field of teaching within the first three years, and in urban districts the attrition rate can soar to a disturbing 30% to 50% in the first year (Salazar, Gudwin, & Nevin, 2008). We know potentially good teachers who leave the field after their first or second year, saying, "I can't do this anymore." One such teacher taught one year at an inner-city school, where all four of the third-grade teachers were new. None of them knew how to help the others, because they were all trying to just keep their heads above water. According to one of them, they felt there was very little support provided to them. That particular new teacher had the potential to be a very successful teacher, but we lost her after the first year.

Spotlight on Javier

When Javier was growing up, all he wanted was to be a teacher. He was enrolled in a dual certification program, and upon graduation he earned his master's in special education and a bachelor's in education. He interviewed at a local middle school in a predominately Hispanic and black, non-Hispanic neighborhood. The school was graded a C according to Florida's A+ Plan, which indicated it was in need of improvement, but not identified as underachieving. He was hired in June for the following academic school year and spent the summer setting up his classroom, spending roughly close to $1,000 before the school year started in making his classroom as inviting as possible. The classroom looked as if it belonged on the cover of a journal indicating what an effective classroom should look like. He had outlined his behavioral plan, had reviewed the district-mandated curriculum, and had attended new teacher orientation, which assists in acclimating new teachers and those new to the district to the climate of the school system, as well as the school climate. On day one, Javier could not have been more excited. He barely slept a wink the night before and was the first to arrive to work, even beating out administration. By day ten, Javier turned in his letter of resignation with the large urban school district.

If Javier would have had a mentor who could lend a listening ear and provide guidance during those critical first two weeks and thereafter, we think it would have made a difference in Javier's career.

JOYS

I still cannot get used to how much my heart soars with every student's success, and how a piece of my heart is plucked away when any student slips away.

—Delissa Mai, ninth-grade teacher, Wyoming (DePaul, 1998).

When a teacher sees the smile on a student's face when she finally "gets it"—that epitomizes the joy of teaching. The successes that come with student achievement are the heartbeat of it all, the reward of a very special profession. According to Joanna,

It was the individual student stories that really inspired me and kept me going. For example, T.—I worried about him all year. I thought about him when I was at home. I constantly thought about his big goals and how I could help him individually, in small groups, and in the whole-class setting. I was willing to do whatever it took, and he showed tremendous growth. He was a concrete example of the unbelievable accomplishment I made as a first-year teacher, that all of my students grew two years in their reading levels. That was my big goal for each of them. I really had high expectations for all, and we accomplished it together.

Earning the Respect of Peers (Sharing What They Learned at the Workshop)

Sometimes new and early-career teachers are so on the ball that they are put in the position of actually sharing knowledge with others at their school or in **professional learning communities** or workshops, even as new teachers. Some are recognized for their teaching practices as "Rookie Teacher of the Year" for their schools or their districts. Some are positively recognized by parents and their peers. One new teacher shared her secret of fitting in and earning the respect of her peers:

I joined in on as much as I could handle. I became the coach of the girls' volleyball team because no one else wanted to, was on a few committees, went to the meetings with a smile on my face; I tried to make a few friends that were real; I made it a point to listen to the other teachers and offer suggestions that I had learned in our classes and as a first-year teacher. At first, I didn't really talk unless I was spoken to, but as the first two months went by, I gained the respect of some of the teachers because I could offer them assistance with their students with disabilities—I have to say that I really could help them out, . . . and that made them see me in a different light. It helped boost my own confidence, too.

Finally, That Feeling Like You Finally Have It Together—"I Can Do This!"

Wong and Wong (1998) describe this time as "mastery and impact," when knowledgeable and skillful teachers achieve success, knowing how to manage their classrooms, teaching effectively for mastery, knowing how to get their students ready for learning, and maintaining high expectations for their students. Sometimes it is apparent with an exemplary new teacher. Moir (1999) refers to it as rejuvenation and reflection, when excitement, a sense of relief, and anticipation of an even better next year occurs.

Mari, a Latina first-year teacher, shares her excitement at the end of the year with jubilant stories of each of her students' achievements and successes, of her classroom management strategies that are working, of an effective lesson where everyone was learning and on task, of her classroom floor-plan arrangements and meaningful centers, the smile stretching from ear to ear, the twinkle in her eyes as she describes Christopher's progress in leaps and bounds. The excitement in her voice tells the listener that she absolutely loves her role as a teacher, that it is so much more than a job, and that she finally has it together and loves it. Her students and their parents also see it, which adds to the reinforcement of being an effective teacher. Sure, she has moments of ups and downs, but a high percentage of them are ups, not downs. She has the feeling of "I can do this!" and it continues to motivate her to maintain that success.

Spotlight on Joanna

What can we learn from a new teacher? Having a dialogue with a successful first-year teacher can teach us a great deal about supporting new teachers. Whether you are a new teacher yourself, a seasoned mentor, an administrator, a university professor, a university student, or a person interested in supporting new teachers, listen to the words of wisdom from a first-year teacher who was recognized as a top "Rookie Teacher of the Year." Joanna was a first-year teacher through Teach for America, the national corps of recent college graduates who commit two years to teach in low-income schools in the effort to expand educational opportunity. She did not have a background in educational pedagogy, but she quickly rose to the top, despite the cultural differences at her school. Assigned to teach in a low-performing school in a large urban setting, she shares some of her joys and tips with us:

Something that helped me during my first year teaching was holding high expectations for all of my students. We were constantly working toward our big goals. My students and I knew what these goals were, as they drove our actions on a daily basis.

(Continued)

(Continued)

Observations by my Teach for America program director helped me, followed by discussions during which we would troubleshoot some problems that I thought I was having. I was truly supported by my first-grade team, but especially by the first-grade teacher next door to me. Our reading coach came to me when I was setting up my classroom and spent hours setting it up with me, making sure I had what I needed for success. She also observed me while I was teaching and gave me positive feedback. I appreciated those noncritical observations and the opportunity to brainstorm solutions for aspects that weren't working. Having honest conversations about teaching benefited both of us.

I had such strong administrative support—it is a big part of my success. My principal was so responsive, encouraging, and very helpful in making sure I was doing all I needed to do.

I met monthly with a support network through Teach for America. We talked about teaching strategies and shared best practices. I also attended professional learning communities at my school. The support in a comfortable setting was so positive.

I constantly reflect on what I do, and I'm hard on myself, so I'm always thinking things could be going better than they are. Self-reflection is what really makes a teacher better. . . . If you're reflecting and really diving into those things that you do every day and thinking critically about them and how to change things that aren't working—that's a huge step toward improving your skills. It's hard to walk into a classroom and be exceptional from the beginning. For instance, I need to get better at breaking my students up in meaningful small groups and planning different remediation activities for when I am working with a small group. I need more professional development on making center activities meaningful and worthwhile, while differentiating the instruction for the low, middle, and high student.

I want to help myself develop better as a teacher. I want to improve my teaching skills so I can really do wondrous things!

Ultimately, my students and I were the ones who connected through the year and the relationships I formed with them and their families are what really helped us to be successful.

Joanna succeeded in doing "wondrous things" with her students. She is one of those phenomenal teachers who, with quality support, outshine all expectations.

MANAGING TIPS

Procedures

Procedures tell us how to function in an organized and predictable manner. Just as we follow procedures in our everyday life, while driving, paying for our groceries at the grocery store, getting gasoline for our car, and getting on the mass transit system, classroom procedures enable us to run a smooth classroom setting, with expectations known.

Procedures for the following situations are essential for an effective classroom (adapted from Wong & Wong, 1998):

- Getting started: the beginning of the class or period routine
- Quieting the class
- Students who need assistance
- Transition
- Movement of students within the class
- What to do with all the papers
- End of the class or period routine
- Changing groups
- Lining up
- Heading a paper
- Starting work immediately
- Handing out and collecting materials or work

Working With Paraprofessionals

Working with paraprofessionals may bring an increased benefit to your classroom, by adding to the cultural understanding of your diverse population and assisting students in need. It may also bring challenges to the new and early-career teacher. Effectively collaborating with paraprofessionals can be a worthwhile endeavor if successfully implemented.

Tips for Working With Classroom-Based Paraprofessionals

- Talk to each other. Build a rapport. A positive working relationship is a plus. Sit down together and chat about your combined goals for the classroom. Communicate your own educational philosophy. Elicit theirs. Listen.
- Clarify the roles and responsibilities of the paraprofessional.
- Find out the strengths and weaknesses of the paraprofessional. Build on those strengths. Use them to benefit the classroom. (One of us had a paraprofessional who was not strong in reading aloud, but with lessons and materials planned in advance, the paraprofessional chose to take the materials home to practice.)
- Plan, plan, plan! Include your paraprofessional's focus in your own lesson plans. Work on them together if that is appropriate. Prepare a copy of the lesson plans for both adults.
- Schedule time effectively and wisely.
- Prepare materials together.
- Respect and appreciate each other.

Parent Conferences

Parent conferences can be an added stressor for new teachers. Jorge had a challenging parent conference during the first two months on the job. He was barely keeping his head above water, yet he knew he needed to present himself as a confident and competent teacher during that conference. He remembered that it was a good idea to start with the positive, have concrete examples ready to share, and be sensitive to the fact that the parents had to schedule their conference around their work. The focus (both of the parents and Jorge) was to help the student, so he tried to be very pleasant. Actually, what Jorge did was follow the *do*s from Table 2.1. How to avoid the stress of a parent conference gone wrong, and how to have a good feeling parent conference: When a positive connection is made with the parents, amid confidence that is joined with the feeling of competence, it is a most joyous occasion. Table 2.1 shares some practical *do*s and *don't*s of a successful parent conference:

Table 2.1   The *Do*s and *Don't*s of Parent Conferences

Do	*Don't*
Have an "action plan" of what you would like to share	Focus on your complaints
Share something positive	Go into the conference cold turkey
Have tangibles to show: work samples, behavior plan, contract	Get defensive
Have notes written on index cards, a notebook, or a composition book; whatever is doable for you	Be negative
Know who is going to attend; if you need assistance, plan ahead	Forget your manners
Call or send a note reminder ahead of time and call or send a note of thanks afterward	Sit at your desk
Accommodate the parents' schedule if at all possible	Make the parents uncomfortable
Decide ahead of time what the best seating arrangement will be	Discuss other students
Offer suggestions and welcome collaboration	Discuss other teachers

Managing It All

How does a new or early-career teacher balance the daunting paperwork, the planning and teaching of lessons, the classroom management, the difficult students, the challenging parents, the administration's demands, the overwhelming stress of student achievement? The recipe for managing it all is equal parts of

- learning how to prioritize;
- being organized;
- collaborating with successful teachers and sharing ideas;

- allowing yourself to work on some of it in the comfort of your home;
- asking for help;
- making the time to meet with other teachers outside of school time, forming relationships, and bonding with those who are successful; and
- reflecting on your practices.

It is a juggling act—and once you find what works, something else may occur, and just when you think you've got it, you have to readjust again! As Joanna states, "I self-reflect on a daily basis; I'm always trying to be a better teacher."

For help in managing it all, we suggest that you keep a journal with pages separated into a T-chart like the one in Table 2.2.

Table 2.2 Managing It All: What Works and What Doesn't

What Works	What Is Not Working
Changes to Try:	

Jot down your thoughts every day. Keep an ongoing reflection of what worked and what didn't. Add your thoughts on what revisions may help. Go back and review often. Fine-tune your teaching practices, sharpen your skills, zero in on what you know needs to change. Think of what your favorite professor in college would think of your day. Pretend you are seeing it from someone else's eyes.

Remember Pierre's voice at the beginning of the chapter? Did you think of some possible strategies for Pierre?

- Collaborate with other personnel at the school site; ask for help from the special education teachers, school psychologist, or social worker for R. He may require more than what you can give him in the academic setting.

- Structure your day with consistent procedures so the students know exactly what is expected of them.
- Look at your classroom environment and setup. Can the chairs and desks be repositioned in a way that would help the students? Maybe small groups of desks clustered with independent work areas would work; that's what we've found most successful with our students. You may want to try it.

Remember Joanna and her reflections? Joanna is a motivated adult learner. She is a prime example of a lifelong learner, of what Joyce and Showers (1995) refer to as the omnivore—the one who devours everything and wants to learn more and more. Hearing the joys and struggles from successful teachers is an avenue by which we can learn about supporting others in the classroom. It can help us plan induction programs. It can also ignite and awaken our own teaching beliefs and practices.

Support to new teachers, particularly from their trusted colleagues, has been shown to be critical to teacher retention. One way of providing support to teachers is through collaborative environments at the school sites. And this has proven to be beneficial to preventing burnout (Billingsley, 2005). According to Salazar, Gudwin, and Nevin (2008),

> Teachers who have a network of support develop a sense of belonging, which is one of the more basic needs in Maslow's Hierarchy of Needs. The sense of belonging is corroborated by Maria's response when she says, "It gave me the structure I was looking for; . . . it gave me the guidance I was looking for. . . . I didn't feel so lonely. . . . I felt like it was a community. I felt a sense of belonging. I don't know if it was because we were all beginning teachers, but it was more like a family, not like I was a stranger. It made a huge difference in my first year of teaching." (p. 54)

Making and maintaining connections, networking, building trust in relationships, maintaining reciprocity—all of these attributes help teachers in bridging the community of educators as we do things with and for each other. The teaching field can be very isolating; however, the magnitude of the effects of social capital can make or break the success of a new and early-career teacher.

For those of us who are mentors, as we listen to the voices of our new teachers, we will continue reflecting on how to provide more effective support and a stronger set of skills. "By helping new teachers build a strong foundation, we are giving back to a profession that has nourished us intellectually, psychologically, and emotionally. By mentoring new teachers, we are brought back to our own first years of teaching when someone may have guided us through the tough times" (Delgado, 1999, p. 29). "And when we go back to our own first years, we are reminded why we went into this profession to begin with . . . to make a difference in a child's life, to teach, to reach, to stretch beyond our wildest dreams" (Gudwin, 2002, p. 49).

Teacher Leaders and Their Roles as Mentors

We cannot hold a torch to light another's path without brightening our own.

—Ben Sweetland

As you read Chapter 3, we encourage you to reflect upon the following questions:

1. What do we need to know about teacher leaders?

2. What can we learn from listening to the voices of mentors?

3. What is the role of a high-quality mentor?

4. What do we do when we don't know what to do?

5. Why is it important to know the stages of development that a teacher experiences?

To help you discover your own understandings of these questions, the content of the chapter is organized in the following sections: Teachers as Leaders, Mentoring, The Role of the Mentor, What Do the Voices of New Teachers Say About Mentors and Their Roles? and What We Now Know. We anchor the content in the context of various scenarios that illustrate teacher leaders and the voice of the mentor.

TEACHERS AS LEADERS

Spotlight on Ms. Perez

Ms. Perez has been teaching special education in the elementary setting for fifteen years. She loves the profession and still wakes up in the morning looking forward to getting to her classroom. She still maintains the enthusiasm of a new teacher, which is coupled with the competent feeling of knowledge that 2,700 days (16,195 hours) of teaching experience has given her. Ms. Perez is a mentor. She is an exemplary teacher who thinks of quality teaching strategies and methods as naturally as she breathes. She is a mentor who loves working with other teachers. This teacher leader exemplifies whom we want to make a difference in the lives of our new teachers.

According to Moir and Bloom (2003), "We have found that mentoring offers veteran teachers professional replenishment, contributes to the retention of the region's best teachers, and produces teacher leaders" (p. 59). Mentoring experiences—the experiences of guiding and leading someone else—can be a foundation for becoming a teacher leader.

Spotlight on Mr. Raul Escarpio

Being a mentor has allowed me to further reflect on my practice in my classroom. As a mentor, Project GATE allows me to hone in on my abilities and think "outside the box" in terms of culturally and linguistically diverse learners. I know that I need to be the kind of teacher that goes that extra mile because that is what I instill in my mentee and want her to learn. It is not about the most creative lesson or the most colorful bulletin boards that will make me a better teacher; it is about caring enough about my students that allows me to be the best professional that I can be. I try to see the mentee as an extension of myself in the field and try to assist her the way I would have wanted to be assisted. It is refreshing to see that she has taken the lead and become independent in her practice. She trusts her instincts and values her creativity. While I would like to think that her growth was a direct result of my actions, I know better. She always had that gift, that sparkle, that light: She just needed the encouragement and validation. If this program provides that confidence and leads to greater retention in the field, then this program has been a blessing. Some would say that our students are our greatest treasure (and deservedly so), but in looking at beginning teachers, they are also our treasure. Without their enthusiasm and passion for students, then education just becomes mechanical and boring. I wish I would have had this program when I began teaching.

Raul, a National Board Certified Teacher in the middle grades content, is a true teacher leader, a mentor and an educator who has so much to offer to other teachers. In his ten years of teaching experience, he has worked in both general education content area and special education. As a Cuban American who teaches in the heart of a largely Hispanic population consisting of 95% Hispanic; 2% black, non-Hispanic; 2% white, non-Hispanic; and 1% Asian/Native American/multiracial students, Raul is able to connect to his students and their parents both culturally and linguistically, as a high majority of this particular Hispanic population is also Cuban American. Raul worked closely with his mentee of Haitian descent, taking into consideration the cultural and linguistic differences that might occur.

As teacher leaders, knowing the cultural rules will assist you in the role of power. For example, as Lisa Delpit (1995) states, "I have come to conclude that members of any culture transmit information implicitly to co-members. However, when implicit codes are attempted across cultures, communication frequently breaks down. Each cultural group is left saying, 'Why don't those people say what they mean?' as well as, 'What's wrong with them, why don't they understand?'" (p. 25). Working with various populations of staff requires teacher leaders to be knowledgeable and aware of intercultural differences. For example, the Hispanic population is a "large and growing" category that is made up of "several ethnic groups, the largest of which are Chicanos, Puerto Ricans, and Cuban Americans" (Martinez, n.d., p. 2). Leadership is a complex cultural process and is different across people. We have found that subgroups of the Hispanic and other populations may be so diverse that it is imperative for teacher leaders to have a working knowledge of cultural differences, even the subtle differences within the same population.

How Do Exemplary Teachers Become Leaders?

Teacher leadership is the process by which teachers, individually or collectively, influence their colleagues, principals, and other members of school communities to improve teaching and learning practices with the aim of increased student learning and achievement.

—York-Barr and Duke (2004, pp. 287–288)

Oftentimes, as is evident in our background work with teachers, teacher leaders are mentored by someone who sees the potential in them. Their mentors may help them fine-tune their leadership roles by guiding them along through the execution of their vision or agenda.

From the Voice of Magda

During my first year of teaching, I embarked on what many would consider an overwhelming amount of additional work and stress. Given the support provided to me by both my parents and a great teacher leader, my mentor and presently my colleague, I decided to pursue my master's degree in reading. My experiences, both professionally and personally, have impacted my role as a teacher leader. During this time, my school was undergoing an application process to receive an esteemed award from the state. Although I did not take on a leadership role immediately, the journey of being considered a teacher leader evolved. How did I develop it? It certainly was not overnight, and it was not an act that I purposefully sought. I became a voice for my students. Gradually, I realized that I possessed the four Cs of leadership, as defined and encouraged by the National Community for Latino Leadership (2001): character, competency, compassion, and community service. I had character and strong moral values, both personally and professionally in regard to understanding, supporting, and advocating for my students with disabilities. As we developed an inclusionary program at my school, I supported the teachers, and they knew that if I said I was going to do it, I meant it. I provided the teachers with instructional practices grounded in research. My work both in the classroom with my students and with my colleagues was of top caliber. Many times, my colleagues regarded me as a seasoned teacher, instead of a "rookie" teacher. I had previous teaching experience in working with students with disabilities in a private prekindergarten program, as well as personal experience as an aunt of a student with disabilities. In addition to my experience and competency, I also possess compassion. My struggles of leaving my native country of Nicaragua, when I was just three, have had a humbling effect on my personality. I am extremely empathetic toward others. I also valued the teachers with whom I worked, because of who each one is as a person. Teaching is not an easy job, and I know through my experiences of working with hundreds of teachers that the decision to become one is rooted in the desire to make a difference. For that alone all teachers should be valued. Lastly, during my first year and my eleven-year career as an educator, I have learned that one of the greatest activities that allow leaders to grow is service to the community. During my first year, I joined the Council for Exceptional Children, at both the local and state levels, as well as the Dade Reading Council and a few other organizations. Through these experiences, I was also given the opportunity to rise to leadership positions to include newsletter editor, conference co-chair, president-elect, and a few others in several organizations. Teacher leaders, particularly of culturally and linguistically diverse backgrounds, will have a significant impact in the educational system, and nurturing and developing teacher leaders is critical.

From the Voice of Denise

During my twenty years in the classroom as a teacher, I was fortunate to have many opportunities provided to me in various leadership roles. Some were initiated by me, and some were offered to me. At the beginning of my career, I did not have a deep-seated desire to be a leader and certainly not an administrator. However, during fifteen years with two wonderfully insightful principals, Ms. Clemencia Waddell and Mr. Fredric Zerlin, I was afforded the opportunity to excel in numerous leadership roles. They opened the door for me, having seen in me a potential I wasn't even aware of at the time. Part of my experiences included being a peer mentor teacher, department chairperson, curriculum leader, committee chair, and officer of such groups as the administrative cabinet, a schoolwide intervention team, and special education team. In my teacher leadership capacity, I was very close to the principal, sometimes his or her spokesperson, and I could see and understand the vision that they had and help pave the way for implementation. Oftentimes I had a certain amount of clout in the culture of the school and was respected by many different groups of teachers and staff. Working in an urban school staffed with multiple ethnicities, I had friends from many different groups who helped me be aware of intercultural differences just by forming interactive relationships with me, not by tutoring me on the ins and outs of cultural differences. According to Moller and Pankake (2006), "the ability to influence other teachers to improve their practice, whether by design or by chance, depends on how teachers view each other in terms of their competency, credibility, and approachability" (p. 26). Having respect in the school culture assisted me in being able to go the extra mile as a teacher leader by having a clear understanding of the work that needed to be done. In the best-case scenario, teacher leadership is a mission that appears to find those capable of handling it—it is a way to spread the message to a larger group of people, thus benefiting both the teachers and their students, and I am fortunate that I was afforded that opportunity, which later on paved the way for my success as an administrator.

Table 3.1 provides a sampling of common characteristics that we found teacher leaders may exhibit. As you peruse the characteristics, reflect on the leaders you personally know and the positive attributes they may exhibit.

Informal and formal leaders are expected to lead. Sometimes it is an expectation by their colleagues as well as administrators. This leadership may be in the form of leading in the classroom, leading in schoolwide curriculum, acquiring knowledge, and sharing that knowledge with their colleagues.

To be most effective, teacher leaders must be aware of the inherent cultural and linguistic differences and address them in their practice. Learning styles as well as cultural differences of teacher leaders must be addressed. For example, Luli, a fourth-grade classroom teacher of fifteen years from Cuba, is very organized, and some may even think she is a bit compulsive. When she shares information with teachers, she is aware that her learning style and personality are different from some of the other teachers, and that she has to tone it down a little bit with a couple of her colleagues, so she does not come across as abrasive and pushy.

As teacher leaders, we need to be aware of our own embedded cultural traditions and reflect upon how our actions as leaders may be impacted by our own cultural backgrounds as well as our awareness of others' cultural differences. Our cultural backgrounds influence the way we react; if we understand and embrace the differences, we will be more effective as teacher leaders.

Table 3.1   Common Characteristics of Teacher Leaders

Teacher leaders demonstrate:		
A desire or interest in leadership, that would have emerged regardless	A hidden talent, but the principal "opens the door" to leadership, seeing potential	The ability to see the end in mind; can see the long run, the potential
The ability to influence others	A close relationship with principal or administration	The ability to speak . . . and people listen
An ability to volunteer, the "do-ers"	Clout in the culture of the school	Open communication with the administrator and staff
A strong character and moral values	A willingness to continue to learn themselves and to share with others	A constant desire to improve teaching practices
Trust in the administrator; if the administrator wanted something, a leader would trust, see the vision, and be able to carry it out	An ability to understand the work that needs to be done and the impact it may have	The saying, "If you want the job done, give it to a busy person"

Teacher leaders are:		
Vocal	Good organizers	Knowledgeable
Part of the core group of worker bees that are known to get the job done	A catalyst for change—they embrace change	Aware of social injustices; an act toward someone or a group of people makes them want to do better, see change
Not into gripe sessions . . . can implement without the whining	Sometimes quiet backstage workers	People who "go the extra mile"
Approachable	Credible	Informal or formal leaders
Compassionate	Competent	Empathic

MENTORING

Now that we have a basic understanding of teacher leaders, we will now expand that concept and discover the specific role of the mentor.

Table 3.2 helps us explore specific ways that mentors can make a difference in the lives of new and early-career teachers, based on the experiences we have had in a large, urban school district.

Table 3.2   If Your New Teacher Says . . .

If Your New Teacher Says . . .	Mentors Can . . .	Focus Discussions and Guiding Questions
"I'm not sure exactly what I'm doing, but I'm ready to dive in and I know I can do it."	• Set up classroom together. • Set up centers, routines, procedures. • Set up student/parent lists for easy access for contacts. • E-mail words of encouragement, a cute poem. • Be available.	• Have you set up your centers? • What are your procedures (such as collecting homework, sharpening pencils, transitioning from one task to another)? • Do you need help with _____? • What's going well?
"I'm overwhelmed."	• Provide a listening ear. • Model a lesson. • Look at options (such as lesson plans) together. • Share Web sites to enhance lessons. • Have curriculum talks. • Provide organizational tips. • Provide concrete ideas about classroom management. • Help prioritize.	• Let's reflect on this . . . • Did you ask yourself what could be done differently? • Have you found a successful way to teach _____? • What can I do for you to make this better? • Are you able to plan and collaborate with other teachers? • How can I help you get prepared for your principal's evaluation?
"After four years of college, I'm ready to throw	• Be a friend. • Take new teacher out to dinner or a social gathering.	• Let's talk about what happened today at _____. • What would help you more feel successful?

(Continued)

Table 3.2 (Continued)

If Your New Teacher Says . . .	Mentors Can . . .	Focus Discussions and Guiding Questions
in the towel. I don't know if I can do this anymore."	• Share sound resolutions to specific problems. • Support; provide a shoulder on which to lean. • Check in frequently. • Connect new teacher with networking groups and blogs for communication with other teachers. • Offer some new classroom management ideas. • Be there.	• Remember to take five or ten minutes at the end of each day to reflect on what worked and what didn't. • Were you able to use the blog or get any information from the networking group? • How's that classroom management plan going?
"I need a break to pull it together." "I'm feeling better— I think I can do this."	• Over winter break, meet together to plan and organize materials. • Celebrate the successes together. • Offer new ideas for lesson plans and activities. • Assist with test prep, test-taking tips.	• What can I do to further prepare you and your students for upcoming testing? • What teaching strategies are most beneficial to your students? • Remember how far you've come! • Were you able to develop long-range planning like the example we reviewed?
"Whew, I made it!"	• Help highlight students who were successful and why, as well as instructional procedures that were beneficial. • Have a celebration dinner and reflect on the good times and not-so-good times; laugh, smile, embrace the successes.	• Reflect upon the things that went well and things that didn't. Enter it into a T-chart to keep as a reference. • What will next year look like? • What do you hope to accomplish during your second year? • Remember this year— your first year is always special.

THE ROLE OF THE MENTOR

After thirty-one years in this profession I continue to learn so much from programs like Program GATE. Over the years, mentoring has taken on many different roles. Seeing the role evolve has forced me to see my role in a different light. Coaching a young colleague and witnessing the growth during the school year are exciting and rewarding. Being provided with the necessary tools and the professional development opportunities prior to being assigned a mentee provided me with a wealth of information.

—Collette Combs, mentor

Supporting new and early-career teachers through their first years of teaching can be challenging as new teachers experience the day-to-day demands and joys of their new profession. Oftentimes, the various roles of mentors mean wearing different hats, as they guide the new and early-career teachers through their phases of development. Mentors are often described as guides, role models, listeners, friends, lifesavers, and much more. Table 3.3 shows a more in-depth look at the various roles.

Table 3.3   The Many Roles of a Mentor

Role	Action
Guide	Guide, direct, lead
Role model	Model lessons in class, act as a role model in situations
Listener	Be an active listener; a real listener, not always to provide advice, sometimes just listening
Friend	Support as a trusted friend, a comrade, a buddy
Counselor	Provide a shoulder to cry on, a hug for feeling better, offer a dialogue of options for resolving issues
Family member	Offer a nurturing, trustful relationship
Lifeline; lifesaver	Be accessible, approachable, knowledgeable
Coach	Offer motivation, instructional coaching, help prepare, give a pep talk when needed
Advisor	Consult, provide advice and feedback
Resource	Provide resources such as professional books, Web sites, blogs, and teacher products
Co-teacher	Act as a colleague, an equal, a peer teacher
Advocate	Support, sponsor; stand up for the new and early-career teacher

In most situations, we have found that mentors learn a great deal from their mentoring experiences. Let's listen to the voices of a few of our mentors of Project GATE, a successful mentoring teacher induction program that was specifically designed for a particular group of teachers, in collaboration with a local state university and an urban school district. Project GATE is discussed more in depth in Chapter 6.

> In order to succeed in today's competitive environment, corporations must create a workplace environment that encourages employees to continue to learn and grow. Project GATE has exceeded this expectation.
>
> I have participated in this program for two years in the capacity of a mentor. Pairing an experienced teacher with a beginning teacher is mainly for the purpose to help the beginning teacher. Through my experience in the program, I also grew and learned from the beginning teacher as they also have new skills that I did not learn in school. For example, I have learned new uses of technology and different strategies that have arisen since my time in school. The communication and learning process has gone both ways between my mentee and me. It has also allowed me to feel very satisfied at helping someone else. When you start off your teaching career, it can be very overwhelming.
>
> Mentoring can be a highly effective means of evoking purposefulness and generating high levels of motivation and teamwork amongst colleagues. In addition, you may even end up developing a lifetime friendship. . . . I have!
>
> —Joy A., mentor

Just as Joy learned new information from her mentee, Rosa also embraced hers as a friend, looking forward to working together for a common goal. Rosa H., a traditional, Hispanic, well-seasoned teacher, shares her thoughts:

> I hope that I have become a trusted friend, a source of information, a good listener, and sensitive to her needs. There are many unique differences at each school. There are different ways to reach the same goal, which is high student achievement. We have worked together to reach that goal.
>
> —Rosa H., mentor

Myleen Quintana reflects upon her mentoring experiences also, focusing on the who, what, and why of supporting a new teacher. Even though mentoring experiences are unique in a way, they also share some connecting threads of similarities, one of those being learning from their mentees. Myleen describes her mentoring experiences in detail:

Mentorship refers to a developmental relationship between a more experienced mentor and a less experienced partner referred to as a mentee or protégé. Project GATE is a *true* mentoring program available specifically for beginning teachers, offering them help and assistance for a successful academic year! This program offers support, guidance, and assistance as the mentee may experience a difficult period, face new challenges, or work to correct earlier problems. Beginning teachers are paired with a more experienced teacher. Mentors are available to answer questions, observe classes, problem solve, and talk confidentially to new teachers about problems they may be facing in the classroom. The purpose of the relationship, ultimately, is not just to support the new teacher, but also to maximize his or her effectiveness in the classroom.

My experience with my mentee has been very rewarding. I have been able to work with my mentee one-on-one, in order to enable her to have a positive, rewarding, and profitable experience through my mentoring. I have also been able to enjoy a beginning teacher's energy and love for teaching. Together we have been able to talk about strategies to assist her with issues such as academics, behavior, and even the dreaded paperwork. As a mentor, I have also been able to learn new ideas from my mentee, and I have to admit her energy and desire to teach are contagious! The experience has also provided me with a newly found friendship and a partnership that will continue through the years. Thanks!

—Myleen Quintana, mentor

Although the roles and responsibilities of mentors will vary somewhat, some conventional roles and responsibilities include the following:

- Attending professional development on mentoring and coaching
- Observing and providing corrective feedback
- Familiarizing the new teachers with information on school and district policies
- Offering ways to properly develop necessary paperwork
- Sharing knowledge on curriculum
- Guiding new teachers on securing resources
- Creating opportunities to parallel plan and co-teach
- Modeling effective practices
- Providing strategies on how to work with parents and advocates

Sometimes mentoring is a combination of any of the above, or it might just be offering a listening ear and a shoulder to cry on, with a pick-me-up hug to get them through the day, the week, the year—all the while transforming the new kids on the block to the teachers they hope to be. Knowing when to wear which hat is a delicate trait that the mentors must possess.

As we have discovered, there is much to learn about effective mentoring by listening to the experiences of the mentors. Some of the experiences include monumental learning from both teacher leaders and their new teachers, some mentoring experiences are a redefining act of validation, and some recharge our batteries, keeping us motivated to remain fresh in the field, serving as an inspiration.

Spotlight on Ms. Cartaya

Let's hear from Ms. Maria Cartaya, a motherly Hispanic educator who took her mentee under her wing and nurtured her through the rough times. Maria works in the heart of a largely Hispanic population where 59% of the family income is less than $49,999 annually, and 87.6% of the school's population falls under "economically disadvantaged." The students are 98.4% Hispanic; 0.4% black, non-Hispanic; 0.5% white, non-Hispanic; and 0.6% Asian; a very high majority of the Hispanic population is of Nicaraguan descent. Although Ms. Cartaya is not Nicaraguan, she is openly able to connect to her students and parents because she is sensitive to the many cultural and linguistic differences that exist within the various subgroups of the Hispanic population.

This year, for the first time, I've had the privilege of being a mentor for a beginning teacher. This uplifting and rejuvenating experience made me look back 28 years ago when I started my teaching career. I vividly recalled my frustration! I came to my school full of hopes and new ideas, determined to make a difference in the lives of my sixth-grade students with learning disabilities. But the reality of what I was faced with was not what I had expected. Bringing positive changes in their lives was not an easy task to be accomplished in a year's term. I felt lonely. . . . I had no one with whom to share my concerns, my difficulties, my dreams, my ideals.

Project GATE has given me the opportunity of developing a wonderful friendship with my mentee, which I hope continues beyond classroom activities. Through our numerous conversations, we have shared new ideas, new teaching practices, collaborative techniques, classroom management skills, and best ways to use accommodation to meet the individual needs of our students, just to mention a few. My mentee had the opportunity to share her difficulties and concerns with me, thus allowing me to reflect on my teaching career and communicate with her the steps I took to overcome similar situations and rise above the occasion. I wish I had this support my first year of teaching!

I came to Project GATE thinking it was time for me to give back to the field of education a fragment of what I had received through the years. I wanted to share my expertise and years of experience with newcomers. But little did I know that mentoring could enrich my teaching career in such a way. This experience allowed me to examine my communication skills with fellow teachers as well as with students and then bring the best practices into the communication with my mentee. It allowed me to observe two excellent teachers (my mentee and the general education teacher in the inclusion class) and get new ideas from their lessons and techniques. I also learned valuable lessons from my mentee's expertise with technology. She taught me about different interactive Web sites used to teach and reinforce academic subjects, and various ways to incorporate technology in our daily teaching activities.

—Ms. Cartaya, mentor

Ms. Cartaya, an exemplary teacher and mentor, took her role very seriously and found the experience to be worthwhile and rewarding. What a marvelous encounter for both Ms. Cartaya and her mentee!

WHAT DO THE VOICES OF NEW TEACHERS SAY ABOUT MENTORS AND THEIR ROLES?

Janeth shares the following, in a passionate discussion about her mentor: "Maria is not only my mentor; she is my guide and friend."

Relationships are formed and oftentimes flourish. As numerous new teachers shared their thoughts with us, the support stands out: Rachel states, "Outstanding support and guidance leads to outstanding teachers." Ms. Malats shares, "She was my support line. . . . I know I was able to learn so much more and grow as a professional with her assistance." Mariela said, "She was like a backbone for me." When new and early-career teachers have mentors who will "be there" to support and assist, who will be those guides and friends, the chance for success in their chosen field of teaching is increased. New and early-career teachers "are encouraged to achieve their goals through interaction within a positive, collegial (but never dependent) relationship" (Brock & Grady, 2007, p. 78).

Anthony, a new special education teacher in a large urban school district, shared the following regarding his mentor:

Let me once again say "thank you" for assigning to me what I know to be the most wonderful, best, top, prime, model, prize, elite, exemplary, cool, astounding, divine, groovy, super (I think you get the point) *mentor* ever. I just hope that I have enough receptacles to store the wealth of information that she provides.

Anthony had a jump-start on his first year of teaching because of his collegial partnership with an exemplary teacher and mentor named Tan Melton. His enthusiasm was evident, and his new bond kept him going.

An exemplary mentor should have a deep understanding of teaching and learning and should be a passionate teacher and learner too. As Robbins (2004) so eloquently states, "We know now that teacher quality is the factor that matters most for student learning. We must be diligent in making plans for mentoring. Precious resources are at stake" (p. 161).

There is much to learn about the roles of a mentor. When looking at mentors and their work, we want to focus on what the new teachers feel about the mentoring experience when they responded to the question, *What mentoring activity did you like the most?* It is evident that the new teachers appreciated the specific support, classroom visitations and observations, feeling that someone was nearby to help, and the feeling of a lifeline nearby. Table 3.4 provides you with specific favorites of mentoring, from the perspectives of new teachers.

Table 3.4 What Mentoring Activity Did You Like the Most?

New Teacher	The Mentoring Activity I Liked the Most
Jennifer Megee	I really appreciated being observed and getting feedback about how to improve.
Claudia Alverez	I liked visiting my mentor's classroom and having her to come and visit me.
Leslie Bienvenu	Going to my mentor's school and watching how the class lessons, paperwork, and student services were managed is what I liked the most of all.
Anthony Symons	I liked the mentor visits and the one-on-one sessions. This gives me honest feedback on my teaching style to include strengths and weaknesses.
Janeth del Rosario Rodriguez	I liked the school-site visits, permanent support, counseling, and companionship the best.
Soraya Fumero	What I liked the most was my mentor being there to teach me the how and what of my job on a day-to-day basis. Even though I had three years' experience from another state, I found that I needed assistance with the paperwork (which is very different). . . . I needed mentoring to provide inclusion services for my students.
Martha Rodriguez	Visiting my mentor at her school, having my mentor visit me, the face-to-face meetings, and the workshops were the best!
Mildred Boveda	I liked having the ability to call someone—at any time—with a question.
Barbara Essinger	I feel I have benefited most from spending two entire days in my mentor's classroom so I could really get a genuine understanding and feel/see the full effect of her classroom structure, management, and academics.
Cristina Ugalde	I liked creating the partnership.
Tina DiBiase	I liked collaboration with my mentor the best.
Karol Pena	Meeting with my mentor for face-to-face meetings at coffee shops, which allowed for practical and less stressful conversation, was what I liked the best.

WHAT WE NOW KNOW

Ms. Cartaya, an exemplary mentor shared with you earlier, stated so beautifully:

> Project GATE has been an instrument to keep me informed about new initiatives in the field of education, upcoming events and professional development, new ideas to motivate students and arouse in them the love for learning, accomplishments of fellow professionals, and innovative methods and techniques. It is a network of professionals who are deeply concerned about children and have the common goal of bringing the best out of each and every one of their students.

There is no doubt in our minds that partnering a new or early-career teacher with an effective mentor can have profound effects on the success of both the teachers' teaching styles—but the professional development and the support provided to both the mentors and the new teachers are critical to that success. New teachers can learn to be more effective teachers if we give them the right tools and ongoing support. We know that well-prepared teachers stay in the field longer and also produce higher student achievement (National Council for Accreditation of Teacher Education, 2006), but let us not forget the mentors; they too need support and the right tools to get the job done. Our mentors *can* take new and early-career teachers to new levels of teaching—the levels of impact are quite evident.

Spotlight on Michelle Coto-Viltre

Michelle, an exemplary mentor, works at a unique setting, a specialized center school in a large urban district where approximately 58.7% of the parent population's annual household income is under $49,999. This specialized school provides educational and therapeutic services to students, 100% of whom are identified as having moderate to severe emotional or behavioral disabilities. Approximately 79.4% of the students meet the criteria for free or reduced-rate lunch, and 83% of the student population is economically disadvantaged. The ethnicity of student membership is 46.7% Hispanic; 34.1% black, non-Hispanic; 18.7% white, non-Hispanic; and 0.6% American Indian/Alaska Native. Her school has not been able to make adequate yearly progress. Both Michelle and her mentee work with middle school–age students who have emotional or behavioral disabilities. Michelle's mentee works at a more typical urban middle school that is 91.3% economically disadvantaged, with 80% of the student population qualifying for free or reduced-rate lunch,

(Continued)

(Continued)

and includes 6.3% of brand-new teachers, with 61% of the student population Hispanic; 37.9 % black, non-Hispanic; 1% white, non-Hispanic; and 0.1% Asian or Pacific Islander; in contrast, only 2.9% of the student population are identified with emotional or behavioral disabilities, instead of Michelle's 100%. Michelle shares her thoughts as a mentor:

When I think back to my first year teaching, my memories are a mixture of feelings of wonderful ignorance and pure panic. I tried to appear and sound authoritative to the students but, in reality, I was terrified of saying too much and allowing my inexperience to show. I wanted to impress my principal and the students with sophisticated lessons and many times could not get them even started because of the manifestation of the behaviors of my students. When I got home from teaching, I collapsed in bed.

Many times, beginning teachers find themselves alone at the bottom of the world's tallest mountain. School districts are working with teacher associations, universities, and others to start mentoring programs to help beginning teachers, veteran teachers in new assignments, and teachers in need of remedial aid to assist them in transit. With hope, the teaching profession as a whole will be able to tackle the obstacles of educating. In my opinion, mentoring also helps to keep talented teachers on the job.

The definition of a mentor is a trusted counselor or guide. Being a mentor has enlightened my teaching career and taught me several things. I believe that the mentoring relationship that was formed provided my mentee with the opportunity to work closely with and learn from my experience. This relationship was shaped by the activities that my mentee and I participated in together. The time that we were able to meet was a necessary part of the mentoring relationship as it enabled mentoring activities such as observation, co-teaching, and lesson planning to take place.

Project GATE has helped to improve practice, learn professional responsibilities, and ultimately affect student learning in a positive way. In addition to being able to provide support to my mentee, it has also allowed me to reflect on practice and helped my mentee work toward the same goal—improving the quality of education. I feel that this program provided for the potential of fostering a collaborative learning environment for teaching. Project GATE allowed for guidance, support, and assistance to the mentee whenever needed. I was able to feel confident that my mentee is a better teacher and has learned to infuse new strategies and behavior management techniques in her classroom. Knowing that I helped another fellow teacher is a great accomplishment.

—Michelle Coto-Viltre, mentor

To be a teacher leader and move in the direction of a mentor can be a very rewarding role, even as it is added to a mentor's full plate of tasks at hand. New teachers have frequently shared with us the difference a mentor made in their lives. Let us continue to fine-tune our roles as mentors and make them even better.

Do You Remember the Spotlight on Pierre in Chapter 2? Let's Recap . . .

Let's look at Pierre's classroom. On his fourth day on the job, as a brand-new teacher, he was faced with challenges head-on that neither he nor his mentor had any idea how to deal with or "fix" for that matter. Pierre's mentor is a highly qualified, National Board Certified Teacher who loves his profession. After day four of the career he thought was his calling, Pierre is ready to throw in the towel. With his bachelor's and master's degrees in hand, he is ready to quit. Can his mentor help him? Can an instructional coaching scenario assist? Put yourself in his mentor Michael's shoes, and decide how you would help Pierre.

Martin Luther King Senior High School is in the heart of a poverty-stricken, metropolitan area, a hard-to-staff school, with 80% of the students living in the public housing neighborhood. The ninth- through twelfth-grade school has a student population of 61% that is eligible for free and reduced-rate lunches. The student population is 1% white, non-Hispanic; 94% black, non-Hispanic; and 5% Hispanic; the teacher population is 22% white, non-Hispanic; 52% black, non-Hispanic; 17% Hispanic; and 0.9% Asian or Native American.

Let's re-read about Pierre's fourth day on the job:

Things happened today that I really don't feel prepared to handle. It's my fourth day teaching. Yesterday there was central office staff at our school, recommending that I rearrange my classroom to make it a more conducive learning environment. It honestly feels like they are all attacking us, but I know they are trying to help. Today, I was scheduled to have a meeting with a group of professionals, including a student advocate and an attorney. That was stressful beyond belief. But it didn't even take place because of what happened thirty minutes before the meeting when the central office staff again observed my classroom. They were nicely dressed, important-looking people. The students were pretty good at first. I was a little nervous with all of them in my room. And then, it all fell apart. There is a special education student placed in my classroom who has some special problems. I don't know if I'm equipped to handle him. I really didn't learn some of these things in college. On his way to the bathroom, he began pulling his pants down. We tried to get him to the bathroom in time because he has this problem, but as he was walking with us to the bathroom, he accidentally hit R. [a student] in the back of the head. R. thought it was Ms. T [another teacher] and he knocked over a desk and hauled himself toward the teacher, knocking her down to the ground, while she toppled into a central office lady, knocking her to the ground as well. R. then began hitting Ms. T all over the place. She started bleeding. Someone pushed the emergency call button, and the office staff said in a totally sarcastic tone, "What is it this time?" We needed her to call 911. Ms. T. was bleeding and managed to stand up, only to faint and fall to the floor again. It took five adults to hold down R. I haven't been trained in how to deal with this type of student. And I'm not sure I want to. . . . What can I do? I just want to quit, but I went to school to become a teacher.

Now, let's look at this scenario again, wearing the hat of a mentor. If you were Michael, his mentor, what advice would you give? How would you help this young teacher? Think about it. . . . There are a couple of pivotal questions. Do the mentor and new teacher have a relationship? Is there trust or mistrust? It takes time, communication, and honesty to build trust, and things can happen during a new teacher's day even before that relationship is strong. In a well-seasoned mentoring relationship, such incidences can even strengthen the bond.

Let's ponder over two possibilities:

Scenario 1:

Michael: I understand that was a real difficult day. Let me suggest the following. Maybe if you spaced the desks differently. . . . Would that help?

Pierre: I don't think so; he really had space to walk through.

Michael: When you take the classroom management class that we signed you up for, they'll have you look at your environment.

Or

Scenario 2:

Michael: I don't know either. I've never been faced with this either. Is there anything we could have done to prevent this? I'm not sure. Maybe we can get some help from someone. . . . Maybe there's a special education teacher who can give us some advice. I'm going to call my friend L.; she will be a great resource for us, I'm sure. I will stick through it with you and help you—I will keep coming back, and we can work on this together. I won't leave you!

Pierre: Hey man, thanks. I do appreciate it. I hope L. can give us some ideas. And I need them fast. I'm at a loss here.

If you were the new teacher, which conversation would better help you? Table 3.5 gives some examples of strategies that the mentor needs to utilize right from the very beginning.

Before a genuine ethos of caring can be developed and implemented on a large scale, educators must identify and understand current non-caring attitudes of behavior (Gay, 2000).

Table 3.5 Setting the Tone: Strategies for the Mentor

Strategies for the Mentor	Real-Life Example
Build trust before you need it!	My first priority is to let you know I am here for you, I will not go running to the principal or anyone else with your concerns unless you ask me to. I believe in the rule "What happens in Vegas, stays in Vegas!" so we can have a trusting relationship
Enter the classroom without an attitude.	I leave my ego at the door. I want you to know that I have experienced frustration during my beginning years, and still do in fact. I am a teacher, just like you.
Know that you can learn something, too.	I don't approach this job as an expert. Although I know some things, I also know that you know some things. In the process, I'll share some of the things I know, but I want you to share your expertise with me as well (Toll, 2005, pp. 55–56).
Be sensitive to the feelings of your new teacher.	I understand how you say you are feeling; how can I help you?
Don't be judgmental.	I am not here to judge you, but to be your right-hand person, your crutch, your guide.
Give concrete examples.	Here, let me show you a behavior contract that might work with Joey. We can use this one or design another one that's better for him—we can work on it together.

As we have addressed the roles of mentors for new teachers, we are reminded that all of us, whatever our position, have had a mentor to guide us along our path at some time or another. We are fortunate to have people in our lives to help us regain our balance when we start to fall. Thank you to each and every mentor out there—know that you are greatly appreciated and that you truly do make a difference.

4

Characteristics of Effective Coaching

Instructional coaches are on-site professional developers who teach educators how to use proven teaching methods.

—Instructional Coaching,
Kansas Coaching Project

As you read Chapter 4, we encourage you to reflect upon the following questions:

1. How do I apply my knowledge and skills of coaching in my repertoire of assisting a new teacher?

2. What are some of the successful ways to include coaching in job-embedded learning opportunities?

3. What does an instructional coach really do?

4. What do I need to know about age, cultural, and linguistic differences to be an effective coach?

To help you discover your own understandings of these questions, the content of the chapter is organized in the following sections: Components of Effective Coaching, Designs for Effective Peer Coaching, The Art of Coaching, and Coaching and Intergenerational and Cultural-Linguistic Differences. We will include coaching experiences that feature successes, challenges, and problem-solving techniques. We anchor the content in the context of various scenarios that illustrate effective coaching.

Spotlight on Mayra

Mayra was a younger Latina mentor, assigned to Aiko, an older, second-career, new teacher of Asian descent. Since Mayra was aware of the differences that age and cultural experiences might have on their relationship, she was always on the lookout for ways to be a better coach. She focused on the positive experiences she observed in Aiko's classroom, providing specific feedback on specific moments. She was able to realize that Aiko was not as comfortable with technology and the use of e-mail as communication and offered assistance on helping her become more technically savvy. Mayra's language vocabulary included words and phrases such as, "Your previous life experiences are valued, and I can see how it helps you in your classroom" and "It's incredible how you are so willing to go the extra mile—your students are definitely benefiting from your great attitude." Mayra was able to be respectful of the cultural differences that were evident in some of their conversations and expectations. For example, when they met after school for a meeting, Mayra made a special effort to be on time, and took in consideration that Aiko was oftentimes introspective, while Mayra tended to be a little on the loud and hyper side. She tried to tone it down a little when they met, without losing her own identity. During coaching lessons when Mayra actually co-taught with Aiko, modeling particular strategies, she was careful not to overpower her, and encouraged her to take the lead when comfortable. Mayra's awareness of cultural and age differences assisted in making this coaching partnership a successful one.

Protheroe (2003) described East and Southeast Asian cultures as showing a strong respect for their elders and discipline, tending to work more efficiently in well-structured and quiet work environments, and tending not to participate unless asked to. These culturally appropriate characteristics may offer a challenge to a peer coach who is not aware of the differences diverse cultures bring to the table. "Culture is like the air we breathe, permeating all we do" (Protheroe, 2003, quoting Trumbell, Rothstein-Fisch, & Greenfield, p. 1). No matter where you live and work, cultural sensitivity needs to be part of your repertoire. For some, it might mean doing research on your own, attending workshops, or reading professional books and journals, and for all, it always means reflecting on our beliefs.

What is mentoring, and what is coaching? First, let's define the relationship between coaching and mentoring. Mentoring includes many roles that we have previously discussed; one of those roles is that of a coach. Coaching is a strategy that a mentor may use to provide more targeted support to the new and early-career teacher. As Chapter 3 focuses on the roles of the mentors, Chapter 4 focuses on the characteristics of coaching. These two chapters go hand in hand, as a connecting thread that is woven throughout this entire book. The goal is to maximize the variety of ways that we can support new teachers. Mentors have many roles, and a basic understanding of coaching will enhance the support to be provided.

COMPONENTS OF EFFECTIVE COACHING

As we concentrate on the skills of coaching, we begin with the components of effective coaching: Beliefs, teaching expertise, coaching skills, establishing relationship skills, content expertise, and leadership skills; the approaches and cultural values of the coach; and the implications of working with a peer—all are critical components of effective coaching.

The coaching continuum may include something as simple as providing friendship and companionship to analyzing teaching and learning strategies, as depicted in Figure 4.1.

Figure 4.1 Coaching Continuum

Offer friendship	Provide a listening ear, a shoulder to lean on	Dialogue and plan together	Troubleshoot, resolve issues	Demonstration of strategies and lessons	Analysis of teaching and learning strategies

Source: Adapted from Joyce and Showers (2002).

The job-embedded learning structure of effective coaching can positively contribute to the learning outcomes of new and early-career teachers. Coaching can increase collaboration and collegiality, improve work performance, and provide a sense of "I can do it."

John Woodard, the Special Olympics Coach of the Year for the State of Florida, describes a bonus of his instructional coaching role as part of his mentoring responsibility with his new teacher: "She was a friend, a colleague; she always greeted me as her 'savior' and said that I was proactive and always with a smile on my face. . . . You never know how you impact people."

Effective instructional coaching is an important partnership that must include all of the following: awareness of multicultural differences; awareness of linguistic differences; dialogue and reflection of professional learning; real-life application in diverse settings; effective communication skills within a diverse community; and sharing knowledge and resources effectively.

Coaching provides teachers yet another successful way to combine teaching and learning in a job-embedded professional learning opportunity. According to Joyce and Showers (2002), the highest impact on the application of new concepts and the achievement of new skills is through coaching, study teams, and peer visits. This method, as compared to attending workshops only, provides a solid impact of learning. Utilizing a combination of the various methods of professional learning, as shown in Table 4.1, demonstrates the comparison of various types of professional learning strategies and the impact on the actual application of new concepts as understood by the new teachers, which can be most beneficial to educators.

Table 4.1 Comparisons of Professional Learning and the Levels of Impact

Comparisons of Professional Learning	Levels of Impact		
	Awareness of Concept, Plus Concept Understanding	Skill Attainment	Applying Knowledge and Problem Solving
Presentation of theory (workshop)	85%	15%	5%–10%
Modeling	85%	18%	5%–10%
Practice and low-risk feedback	85%	80%	5%–15%
Coaching, study teams, and peer visits	90%	90%	80%–90%

Source: Adapted from Joyce and Showers (2002).

As Table 4.1 shows, to obtain skill attainment and application of knowledge and problem solving, Joyce and Showers (2002) focus us on the higher percentage of impact when utilizing coaching, study teams, and peer visits.

The coach's role includes navigating the new and early-career teacher through reflective conversations about student work, teaching, and learning. The instructional coach guides new teachers in becoming more purposeful about their practice by reflecting on lesson planning, teaching, and student assessment. Effective coaches purposefully wear various coaching hats to help new teachers in becoming stellar teachers (Dunne & Villani, 2007). We know that effectiveness of teachers is the bottom line, where the rubber meets the road. "Research indicates that the effects of well-prepared teachers on student achievement can be stronger than the influences of student background factors, such as poverty, language background, and minority status" (Darling-Hammond, 1999, p. 39).

DESIGNS FOR EFFECTIVE PEER COACHING

Peer Coaching

Peer coaching includes observing, collaborating, and conferencing in a nonjudgmental way, while building a safe and supportive rapport with our peers. Peer coaching often gives new teachers a lifeline of support, while providing mentors the opportunity to make a positive difference in the life of a colleague. Let's highlight some of the effective methods of working with our peers in the various roles of an instructional coach, which may or may not include co-teaching. We will continue this discussion in Chapter 7, to include study groups, instructional data discussions, and professional learning communities within the framework of professional development.

Co-Teaching

Teachers across all levels and subgroups of teaching are exploring new ways to collaborate and deliver instruction to diverse groups of students. Co-teaching with a more experienced coach is one way to provide beginning teachers with the opportunity to reflect upon a shared teaching experience within an atmosphere of mutual trust and respect. Co-teaching is a vehicle to expand collaborative efforts among and between a new teacher and a coach. Coaching occurs when the coach observes, models, and guides the new and early-career teacher during the instruction of the students. Co-teaching includes wearing the hats of both instructional specialist and classroom support personnel, as the role of the coach expands to meet the needs of the new teacher.

In co-teaching, there are many actions that the teams take before, during, and after teaching that lend to powerful personal and professional growth for both the new and early-career teacher and the coach. Aracelys was in her first year of teaching. Upon the recommendation of her mentor, she made daily entries in a journal as a reflective practice. Occasionally Aracelys shared her journal with her mentor, but mostly its purpose centered on reflective journaling for her own growth. Aracelys is from Venezuela. From an early age, her mom instilled in her respect for her elders. In teaching, she had her own ideas, but did not feel comfortable sharing them with an older, more experienced teacher and wasn't sure that Badriyyah would even listen to them. Badriyyah was in her thirteenth year of teaching and had numerous teaching awards. Badriyyah came to teaching with previous experience in her native country of Jordan. They had very little in common, except their passion for student achievement. They knew the benefits of co-teaching for the students, but when they began the school year, they were uncertain of the benefits of co-teaching for each other.

Aracelys reflects on her co-teaching experience:

> At first, I was terrified knowing that someone was going to be in the room with me. Although we had planned for the lesson together, I was nervous that I would freeze up. However, I knew Badriyyah. Badriyyah was the best coach I could have. She had knowledge of a multitude of instructional strategies. I had the confidence in the safety of our relationship. I think that's essential in making co-teaching possible for any team.

Much of the research on co-teaching focuses on a special education teacher and a general education teacher. However, it should not be limited to that situation, and much is to be said for the benefits of expanding the concept of co-teaching to include a coaching relationship in many other teaching situations.

THE ART OF COACHING

As two teachers observe each other's teaching, effective coaching includes providing feedback and assistance, maintaining teaching and content expertise, modeling of techniques and strategies, establishing relationship skills, and demonstrating respect for each other, as well as exhibiting positive collegial leadership skills. As you fine-tune your own coaching skills, complete the Self-Assessment for Effective Coaching in Table 4.2. We feel that as you strive to be the best instructional coach you can be, this reflective assessment will help guide you in your journey.

Table 4.2   Self-Assessment for Effective Coaching

To be used as a reflective piece for mentors, in their role of a coach 1 = disagree; 2 = somewhat disagree; 3 = I don't know; 4 = somewhat agree; 5 = agree	
	I am comfortable with my skills as a teacher.
	I connect well with people; I am a "people-person."
	I have a bank of resources that I utilize.
	I have time to devote to a peer.
	I look forward to working together in a team or partnership.
	I understand my state's standards and can support my peer with curriculum.
	I have exemplary evaluations from administration of my own teaching.
	I have experience with classroom instruction and classroom management.
	I welcome diversity.
	I understand the differences of various ethnic groups.
	I have friends of different races and ethnicity.
	I know about effective communication skills.
	I am a good listener, and I can listen without interrupting or offering advice.
	I value individual differences.
	I know the differences in personality and age groups that exist.
	I am willing to learn about coaching.

(Continued)

Table 4.2 (Continued)

	I understand that I differ from my colleagues and that is okay.
	I can define my culture.
	I am willing to learn about other cultures.
	I do not make judgments about people based on how they look or sound.
	I truly respect people for who they are.
	I know about body language and how important mine is in the role of a coach.
	I am willing to learn about my peers.
	I like to take the time to get to know my peers.
	I understand that communication is an important aspect of coaching.
	I understand confidentiality, and I support it.
	I have a working understanding of differentiated instruction, and I use it myself.
	I have an understanding of the expectations of a new teacher.
	I am willing to co-plan, have deep conversations, observe, co-teach, and problem solve with my new teacher.
	I am a reflective teacher; I reflect daily on my own effective teaching practices.
	I know my own strengths and weaknesses.
	I am aware of the stages of development that new teachers experience.
	I know how to build relationships.
	I am good at providing constructive yet positive feedback.
	I welcome my new teacher to observe me teaching in my own classroom.
	I know what excellent teaching looks like.
	Student achievement is important to me.
	I consider myself an effective teacher.

Table 4.2 gives us a way to focus our reflection of ourselves in the role of a coach. Use this to learn more about yourself as a coach, and let it open the door to further reflection and dialogue.

According to Killion and Harrison (2006), successful coaching includes knowledge and skills in the following areas:

- Understanding the concept of adult learning
- Building trust
- Gaining entry
- Gathering data
- Providing feedback
- Communicating effectively
- Providing support
- Accessing resources
- Facilitating learning
- Expanding content knowledge

The above coaching skills are critical to the instructional coach for the success of the coaching relationship. In addition, a good coach needs to have high expectations and be able to provide positive and guiding feedback in a caring and compassionate way.

Jennifer Abrams, professional developer and national consultant, in a Miami, Florida, presentation to literacy coaches (2008), described author Jim Knight's nine roles of classroom instructional coaches:

1. Market their services

2. Analyze teachers' needs

3. Observe classes

4. Collaborate on interventions

5. Prepare materials

6. Model

7. Observe

8. Feedback-model-observe-feedback

9. Build networks for change

In addition to the necessary knowledge and skills as indicated by Killion and Harrison (2006) and the roles discussed by Abrams (2008), it is obvious that wearing the numerous hats of an instructional coach can be a challenge. Table 4.3 provides some practical and concrete do-and-don't ideas.

Table 4.3 Do This! Not This!

Do This!	*Not This!*
"Let's try this . . ." or "How can I help you?"	Instead of "You need to . . ."
"Since you are the expert of your students . . ."	Not "You haven't been working long enough to know . . ."
Put the new teacher at ease	Not on the defensive
Offer positive feedback	Not in a reprimanding manner
Demonstrate to the new teacher that you'll be there and you're there to stay by keeping your meeting times and being available via phone and e-mail	Don't change your appointments, ignore phone messages or e-mails, or not respond to questions
Provide consistency	Don't be haphazard about your assistance—random help and unsystematic coaching will not be helpful
Build rapport and trust in a sincere manner, being aware of your body language, tone of voice, and interactions	Don't assume rapport and trust will just happen and no one cares if it doesn't
Try to find a connection with each other	Instead of just keeping the relationship as coach and teacher
Focus on the person	Rather than the things that need to be done
Be respectful, acknowledging the other person's opinions	Not condescending, discourteous, or disrespectful
Listen	Instead of always asking questions

COACHING AND INTERGENERATIONAL AND CULTURAL-LINGUISTIC DIFFERENCES

As we move to and from the various hats that we wear in the roles of instructional coach, data coach, role model, and learning facilitator, we must continue to be sensitive to both the cultural and linguistic diversity as well as the diversity in coaching various ages of teachers.

What might new teachers of different age groups want from their coaching experience? What might new teachers of various cultural groups want from their coaches in regards to their learning styles? According to Abrams (2008), there are specific differences in working with people of various ages.

If the new teachers are Nexter/Millennials (born between 1981 and 2000), the following characteristics in their coaches may be a priority for them:

- Comfortable with e-mail communication
- Doesn't patronize; acknowledges their intellect even though they are younger
- Sees the new teachers' growth
- Willing to collaborate and change their own thinking
- Acknowledges the whole life of the new teachers and understands that more exists for them than just the school day

If the new teachers are Gen Xers (born between 1961 and 1980), the following characteristics in their coaches may be a priority for them:

- Constant face-to-face interaction is not needed
- Understands and believes in the life-work balance
- Open to answering "why" questions
- Does not take bluntness personally
- Holds clear discussions, discusses consequences honestly
- Is okay with minimal schmoozing and more of just getting down to business
- Understands that teachers need to get the work done and that there are other priorities in life

If the new teachers are Boomers (born between 1944 and 1960), the following characteristics in their coaches may be a priority for them:

- High expectations for "us"
- Connects with the deep values around education
- Acknowledges and values prior experience
- Understands that personal connections matter
- Knows that "we" is an important concept to the greater goal
- Language used is respectful
- Willing to go the extra mile
- Understands the different position of being a rookie again
- Understands the challenges of the second- (or more) career teacher

In addition to age differences, cultural and linguistic differences are important to consider. For example, Axtell (1998) indicates that, in some Asian countries,

great respect is afforded the elderly, so it is important to let your actions reflect this. Speak to them first. Hold doors open for them. Rise when they enter a room. Give up your seat if no others are available. One gesture of special respect for the elderly is to cover your left fist with your right hand, raise both hands to your breasts, and bow your head with eyes downcast. (p. 205)

According to Irvine and York (1995), there are cultural differences that may need to be considered when working with educators of diverse backgrounds. For example, they characterized Hispanics as those who are holistic and relational learners, who prefer group learning situations, and for whom working one-on-one may be a challenge. We caution against stereotyping bias; however, the characteristics in Table 4.4 are possible learning styles to consider.

Table 4.4 Learning Styles and Cultural Differences

Possible Learning Styles for Learners of African American Heritage	Possible Learning Styles for Learners of Latino Heritage	Possible Learning Styles for Learners of Native American Heritage	Possible Learning Styles for Learners of Asian Heritage
• May be global learners • May prefer whole instead of isolated parts • May prefer inferential reasoning instead of deductive reasoning • May focus on people rather than on things • May prefer kinesthetic and active instructional activities • May prefer evening rather than morning learning • May choose social over nonsocial cues	• May prefer group learning situations • May be sensitive to the opinions of others • May remember faces and social words • May be extrinsically motivated • May learn by doing • May prefer concrete representations to abstract ones • May prefer people to ideas	• May prefer visual, spatial, and perceptual information rather than verbal • May prefer learning privately rather than in public • May watch and then do, rather than employ trial and error • May have well-formed spatial ability • May prefer small-group work • May favor holistic presentations and visual representations	• Decisions may be made with the group in mind • Often show great respect for elders, even in the workplace • May need encouragement to speak their opinions • May prefer small-group work • May need to be encouraged to ask questions

Source: Adapted from Irvine and York (1995), Dresser (2005), and Axtell (1998).

As we explore the differences of cultural background while coaching our teachers, we must continue to consider what it means to work effectively in a culturally responsive manner. Gay (2000) focuses on working specifically with students, but we may want to expand her guidelines in working with teachers in a coaching environment. The important components in a culturally responsive atmosphere include maintaining awareness of cultural knowledge, tuning in to prior experiences, and being aware of performance styles. How do we do this? By acknowledging the cultural heritages of our various ethnic groups, building bridges between home and school, using a wide variety of strategies combined with learning styles, and incorporating multicultural information and resources. "Cultural diversity is a strength—a persistent, vitalizing force in our personal and civic lives" (Gay, 2000, p. 14).

In the role of a coach, we have the opportunity to pave the way for success. At times we are like an athletic coach—the motivator, the pep talker, the "let's practice it, let's get it right" person. Sometimes we are the teacher, partner, friend, equal, and peer. But above all, we are great listeners, each one a partner who is there in time of need, a shoulder to lean on, and a role model of what an exemplary teacher looks like.

5

Communication

What you do speaks so loud I cannot hear what you say.

—Ralph Waldo Emerson

As you read Chapter 5, we encourage you to reflect upon the following questions:

1. What are the secrets of successful communication in the context of quality mentoring programs?

2. What do you most need to know about unique communication patterns of teachers in urban school districts with significant populations of children and their teachers who are from culturally and linguistically diverse families?

3. How can you enhance your relationships with people from other cultural and linguistic heritages who might feel isolated and rejected by the professional culture of schools?

To help you discover your own understandings of these questions, the content of the chapter is organized in the following sections: Intercultural Communication, Nonverbal Communication, Listening in Intercultural Settings, Intergenerational Differences in Communication, Written Communication, and Intercultural Communication and the Standards of the Profession. We anchor the content in the context of various scenarios that illustrate communication barriers and facilitators.

INTERCULTURAL COMMUNICATION

Spotlight on Alexandra

Alexandra is a brand-new teacher from the Caribbean Islands who is working two jobs just to pay her bills. Listen as she describes her experiences to her mentor, in the lilting cadences of her Caribbean English. "The other teachers are so detached from me that they didn't even ask who you were," she lamented. "I feel very alone sometimes and wish for more **camaraderieship** [sic] here."

Wishing for more *camaraderie* communicates a powerful need for connection. Beginning teachers often feel isolated, unlike Barbara, an early-career teacher who discovered from her mentor that frequent communication was critical to her development as a teacher.

However, communication is prioritized differently based on individual differences. Listen to Latanya, a young black, non-Hispanic experienced exemplary teacher, as she describes her experiences during a districtwide teacher planning day, which had been set aside by the school district for teacher preparation.

Spotlight on Latanya

Latanya enthusiastically told her best friend at lunch that day: "I can't believe I've been here since 7:30 this morning and it's 12 noon, and I haven't gotten any work done!"

Latanya was slightly frustrated at her lack of accomplishment, but that morning, she had chosen to use her time to socialize. It is an integral part of her day. Latanya is an exemplary teacher, one who reported to work a week before anyone else did just to set up her classroom—a literacy-rich classroom with at least 1,000 (yes, 1,000!) children's books. Latanya is the kind of teacher who stays at work until 8 p.m. to make sure she is ready for the next day. Interacting socially with her co-workers before focusing on the tasks at hand is a critical aspect of her communication style.

If you were Latanya's mentor, or her supervisor, and if you were not aware of her communication preferences, might you judge her differently? In fact, Singh and Stoloff (2003) explain that many factors can contribute to misinterpretations: choice of words, body language, proximity to each other, tone of voice, or the timing of the conversation.

In Miami-Dade County Public Schools, teachers and students from ninety-eight different cultures and linguistic heritages interact on a daily basis, all within the professional culture of schooling. For some teachers, intercultural communication has become second nature where respect and rapport happen seamlessly. Meet Martha and Janis, as an example.

> ### Spotlight on Martha and Janis
>
> Martha, a Latina woman, chose education as her second career. She jumped from new teacher to an accomplished early-career teacher and started her second year of teaching with confidence, as she was recognized as Rookie Teacher of the Year at her school site. Janis is a seasoned teacher of European descent with over twenty years of classroom experience. Culturally speaking, she is very different from Martha. However, because the support was so strong and partnerships were made with others grouped at the school, the intercultural communication did not appear to be a challenge.

Perhaps Janis and Martha benefited by knowing that Janis, as a representative of the Anglo culture where people are oriented toward individualistic values, tended to focus on task completion as a priority over concerns about personal relationships (as suggested by Singh & Stoloff, 2003). In contrast, Martha, as a representative of the Latina/Latino culture, tended to put personal relationships ahead of tasks. Like Latanya, Martha preferred to interact socially with her colleagues before settling down to tackle the work. Protheroe (2003) discusses these traits as common among African Americans and Latinos in general. Knowing there are individual differences within cultures, it is important to be aware of cultural values on personal and social relationships.

> ### Spotlight on Aurora and Marielena
>
> Two teachers shared the following experience: Aurora, a **Nicaraguana**, is **bilingual/biliterate** (Spanish/English) and is speaking with her colleague Marielena, a Colombian, also bilingual/biliterate (Spanish/English). They sprinkled their conversations with Spanish and English phrases. However, when Aurora used the phrase "Nicoya," referring to a third colleague, Marielena was puzzled that Aurora was calling their friend "Nicoya," because that word has two very different meanings in their respective countries. "Why did you call her that?" Marielena didn't understand why "Nicoya" was used. It just didn't make sense.

What could have happened without clarification? Sometimes there are subtle communication barriers that are unintentionally crossed. However, they have the potential to sabotage interpersonal relationships. The Online Urban Dictionary (2009) includes the definition of Nicoya as meaning *from Nicaragua* but also the derogatory slang meaning of *poor*, as in "wealthy-looking pirate ship containing no gold at all." Researchers such as Chamberlain, Guerra, and Garcia (1999) have identified that cultural dynamics are often not visible: "Social norms for conversation patterns often vary by culture" (p. 4).

Fortunately, both Aurora and Marielena were continuously learning of the cultural and linguistic differences between the multiple cultural groups that existed in their school district. They discovered that a particular Spanish word might be perfectly acceptable to a person from Central America but is considered to be a slang word, even a rude word, to a person from South America. Both Aurora and Marielena experienced the common phenomenon that occurs between culturally diverse people who work in a multicultural setting.

Table 5.1 shares some *Always* and *Never* tips for intercultural communication, which may assist you in your own communication with others.

Table 5.1 What to Do *Always* and *Never* in Intercultural Communication

What to Do **Always** in Intercultural Communication	What to Do **Never** in Intercultural Communication
Always be reflective in the way in which we use verbal communication.	Never send negative messages.
Always think of how the other person is receiving your message—are there any mixed messages going out?	Never assume that your partner understands what you mean.
Always be aware of intercultural differences that may need attention.	Never use intercultural remarks that could be interpreted as rude.
Always listen with an open mind.	Never let your negative nonverbal cues show.
Always try to keep communication open.	Never assume that all Hispanic/Latinos (or members of any cultural group) have the same traditions, language, or heritage.
Always err on the side of too much communication instead of not enough.	Never let a misunderstanding go without clarifying.
Always keep negative messages out of the communication.	Never cut your partner off with your own stories when you are supposed to be listening.
Always build trust through language.	Never believe that your own culture, language, traditions, or belief system is the only one that's real.
Always pay attention to your nonverbal cues.	Never allow cultural differences to get in the way of your trust building.
Always clarify if you are not sure.	Never think that communication won't be worth the extra effort needed to enhance your mentoring relationship.

NONVERBAL COMMUNICATION

Sustained and meaningful communication with groups of people from culturally and linguistically diverse heritages can lead to improved educational practices (Nevin, Harris, & Correa, 2001), but it takes more than words! Pitton (2000) explains that an intercultural dialogue process involves both words and nonverbal signals:

> It's not what you say but how you say it. . . . Nonverbal signals include facial expressions, vocal tone, inflections, and body stance. People often pay more attention to these signals than to the words. Looking away may be interpreted as not being sincere. Frowning while saying I'm glad you came by may be interpreted as not being happy to see you. Sending contradicting verbal and nonverbal signals is a common cause of miscommunication. If the tone matches what is said, it is thought to be believable. (p. 30)

Pitton's remarks remind us that only 10% of any communication exchange is represented by our spoken words. Nonverbal components and body language communicate 60% of all meaning. These include our posture, the gestures we use, the proximity of the teachers, our facial expressions, and even the muscle tension that is seen in our face and necks. Sounds, such as tone, sighs, clicks, snorts, or other indications of sympathy, disgust, or other emotions, that we make while talking represent 30% of all meaning. Have you ever watched people break out in red splotches on their necks and shoulders when upset? What happens to you when someone starts a conversation with a scowl on her face? How do you interpret a person who listens to you while he sighs and very subtly moves his head from side to side? What judgmental decisions do you make when a person clenches a fist or slaps the table when emphasizing a point?

Spotlight on Tina and Carolyn

Tina noticed that the new teacher, Carolyn, with whom she was talking, seemed to be saying words that were positive but her fists were clenched, and she sighed audibly throughout the meeting. In response, Tina became upset and developed red splotches on her neck and shoulders. The nonverbal communication from both people clearly indicated that miscommunication was occurring.

Becoming aware of our nonverbal communication will help ensure that others hear our message as we intended to be heard. We also need to read the nonverbal communication of others to better understand what they are trying to communicate. Later in the year, Tina was able to tell Carolyn that when she became upset, she developed red splotches. Carolyn looked surprised and said, "Oh! I can remember the first time I noticed that! I was so nervous that day that I had to hold my hands tightly closed so you wouldn't notice how much they were sweating, and I kept taking these deep breaths so that I could stay calmer!" But these nonverbal cues can so easily be misinterpreted.

Reflect again on the opening quotation from Emerson: *"What you do speaks so loud I cannot hear what you say."*

You are mentoring teacher-to-teacher. The new teacher whom you are mentoring stated, "I don't think I can deal with these students." You respond by using the active listening tool of restatement, using the mentee's words: "You don't think you can deal with your students. . . ."

What would happen if you said those same words with a different tone of voice and nonverbal gesture? First, imagine that you say it timidly, with a deep sigh. Then imagine that you say it assertively, at the same time you point an index finger. Then imagine that you say it in a helpful tone of voice, with hands open and a slight smile on your face. Then say it in an angry tone of voice with a scowl and clenched fist. Finally, say it in a condescending tone of voice, raise your eyebrows, and have a smirk on your face. Now put yourself in the shoes of the new teacher. What messages would you be receiving from your mentor? Imagine that there are language and cultural differences between the two of you. How might the messages become even more misunderstood?

Peter F. Drucker (1909–2005) was an influential writer whose ideas and work influenced a wide range of people including Winston Churchill and Bill Gates. What do you think about this advice from Dr. Drucker? "The most important thing in communication is hearing what isn't said." What are acceptable gestures; what does eye contact, proximity, and silence mean to different cultures? For example, in some Asian cultures, making eye contact and close proximity may be viewed as a sign of disrespect. What type of feedback is acceptable? As lifelong learners, we must continue learning about different cultures.

LISTENING IN INTERCULTURAL SETTINGS

Listening is powerful and effective only if it is authentic. Stone, Patton, and Heen (1999) suggest that authenticity means that you are curious and you care, not just because you are supposed to. The issue then is this: Are you curious? Do you care? How do you communicate care and curiosity in intercultural settings? Does one culture's expressions of caring become interpreted as being intrusive by another culture? Does one culture's polite treatment of you become interpreted as not caring?

As we build trust within our intercultural relationships, some behaviors can assist in creating a trusting atmosphere. For example, pay attention to the speaker. Listen with your whole body (head tilted slightly toward the speaker, eyes oriented toward the speaker without staring, hands off the computer or keyboard or text-messaging system). Acknowledge the speaker by responding appropriately.

The 3 Cs and an E: Approach to Intercultural Listening

In building interpersonal communication skills for a multicultural setting, four types of communications can tell the speaker you are hearing the messages. In Table 5.2, we suggest that you use the *3 Cs and an E* approach: Clarify, Check perceptions, Concrete examples, and Express empathy.

Table 5.2 Three Cs and an E

Communication Skill	What Does It Mean?
Clarify	The listener asks clarifying statements or questions that help to gain further information about what the other person is thinking, so as to have a better idea about the meaning of the speaker's statement; for example, *"Did you mean that _____?" "What I hear you saying is _____."*
Check perceptions	The listener checks perception of the speaker's emotional context by asking how the speaker may be feeling emotionally; for example, *"How did that make you feel?"*
Concrete examples	When the listener makes statements that refer to specific events or observable behaviors, the listener is anchoring the communication in a concrete example that someone can see, touch, and feel.
Express empathy	When the listener makes statements that identify with and express an understanding of the feeling or situation that is being described by the speaker, the listener is expressing empathy. Empathy can be effectively communicated even when the listener uses clichés such as sympathetically nodding the head and saying, *"Been there, done that!"* or *"As the saying goes, . . . I understand what you are feeling, what you are going through."*

To further assist you in a better understanding of effective intercultural communication interactions, Table 5.3 will provide you with tips that we found worthwhile in our experiences of building and, very importantly, maintaining effective communication.

Table 5.3 Tips for Effective Intercultural Communication Interactions

✓ YES, I Will Use This Tip!	Communication Tip
✓	I will remember what the challenges were during my own first years of teaching—I will be that caring ear.
✓	My job as an authentic coach is to "speak and listen to them as if it is the most important conversation I will ever have with this person" (Kee, 2006, p. 1).
✓	If I want the best from my teacher, I will speak to him as if he is doing his best!
✓	I will keep my nonverbal cues in check—I will notice if I am smiling, frowning, making noises; I will be aware if I have my arms folded or my hands open or clenched.
✓	I will be aware of my posture, the gestures I use, and my facial expressions while communicating.
✓	I will be aware of cultural diversity, traditions, and linguistic differences in multicultural relationships.
✓	I will be aware of my listening skills in an intercultural session.
✓	I will learn the differences that exist between the cultures of the teachers with whom I work.
✓	I will use the 3 Cs and an E approach and clarify statements to help gain information, check perceptions of the speaker's emotional context, provide concrete examples anchoring the communication, and express empathy while listening, all of which will assist in positively building interpersonal communication skills.
✓	I will be aware of generational differences that may occur in the teacher partnerships, knowing that the generational differences may influence the way my partner thinks and responds.
✓	I will use various ways of communication, including verbal and written.
✓	If my partner likes e-mail communication, I will use this mode of communication, matching the "fit" of my partner.

INTERGENERATIONAL DIFFERENCES IN COMMUNICATION

A different type of intercultural communication challenge can be experienced when the communicators come from different generations! Generational differences show up between mentors and beginning teachers. For example, mentors and novices alike may be in their early twenties or may be career switchers.

Dr. Morris Massey (1980) shared a concept that still rings true: "I am who I am because of where I was when I was 10–15 years old." His value dispersion theory points out that individuals within each generation can adopt different values. Even when people are of the same age bracket, not all people have the same outlook. If you asked your colleagues, "What was going on when you were between the age of ten and fifteen?" they will typically note those events, heroes, movies, and the music they experienced. If they then compare their answers, they are typically amazed!

Differences between the generations influence the way that an individual thinks about family life, career choice, balance between the two, and outlook about the future. Given that many people are working longer than in years past and often move on to new jobs after their retirement, it is possible that an educator from a younger generation can become the mentor for someone from an older generation. In enhancing communication between mentor teachers and beginning teachers, awareness of generational differences can make communication more effective.

In what ways might this information on inter- and intragenerational differences enhance intercultural communication? In the Miami-Dade County Public Schools, we've noticed that as many as four generations of educators can be employed as teachers in the same school! In the following table, characteristics of each of these generations are described, including their values and ways to build on their strengths. We've adapted material from Rutherford (2005), *The 21st Century Mentor's Handbook: Creating a Culture for Learning,* to illustrate two dyads.

For each of the two pairings described below, imagine that you are a coach for the mentor-mentee team. Consider what you know about the differences that might occur within and between the generations, and then reflect upon the advice you might offer on effectively communicating with each other in a mentor to new teacher relationship, being sensitive to age and generational differences:

Spotlight on a Traditionalist New or Early-Career Teacher (Second- and Third-Career Educators) and a Millennial Mentor

What advice would you offer to build an effective intercultural relationship for this partnership? Did you notice whether you focused on content (words) or nonverbal gestures or tone of voice? What did you suggest with respect to the differences that might exist if there is another dimension of difference such as linguistic heritage (for example, a traditionalist who is monolingual)?

New Teacher List	Mentor's List
Traditionalists (1920–1942)	**Millennials (Nexters/Gen Y) (1981–2007)**
Events, Trends, and Technology:	Events, Trends, and Technology:
• Pearl Harbor • Stay-at-home moms • Listened to radio • World War II	• 9/11 • Oklahoma City Bombing • Columbine School Massacre • It's all about the *"bling, bling."*
Values and Characteristics:	Values and Characteristics:
• Privacy • Hard work • Respect authority	• Time with family • Diversity • Technology and autonomy
Building Communication From Their Strengths and Life Experiences:	Building Communication From Their Strengths and Life Experiences:
• Acknowledge and ask about their experiences. • Be explicit about the ways they make a difference in their class.	• Send them an e-mail or text message to ask how they are doing or when providing praise. • Provide feedback, as many view silence as disapproval.

Spotlight on Gen Xers New or Early-Career Teacher and Baby Boomer Mentor

What advice would you offer to facilitate effective intercultural communication for this partnership? Sometimes our differences are subtle and sometimes not. Being sensitive to our strengths, weaknesses, characteristics, and values provides a path to more effective communication.

New Teacher List	Mentor's list
Gen Xers (1960–1980)	**Baby Boomers (1942–1960)**
Events, Trends, and Technology:	Events, Trends, and Technology:
• Shuttle *Challenger* disaster • Watergate • *Sesame Street* • Operation Desert Storm	• Vietnam • Civil Rights Movement • Woodstock • Three TV channels
Values and Characteristics:	Values and Characteristics:
• Entrepreneurial spirit • Independence • Creativity and feedback	• Competition • Change • Teamwork
Building Communication From Their Strengths and Life Experiences:	Building Communication From Their Strengths and Life Experiences:
• Let them know they are right on track and give them space to work independently. • Encourage them to use their technology skills in the classroom.	• Offer them opportunities to be involved in the school. • Offer guidance on the desired results: new instructional practice.

WRITTEN COMMUNICATION

Smylie (1994) suggests that conditions to best encourage teacher learning are evident where teachers work with and learn from each other on an ongoing basis in open communication. One way to encourage open communication is through e-mail. E-mail communication is an important vehicle for professional development for teachers, with the fast-growing use of computers. The availability of computers enables communication on an unprecedented scale. The potential for electronic communication in the form of e-mail suggests that teachers can form a network of support, and with these networks new opportunities for professional growth exist, which encourage collaborative professional growth. According to Grunberg and Armellini (2004), e-mails may support the formation of communities of highly committed teachers where seeking and sharing professional resources are accepted as daily occurrences of teachers. E-mail communication allows teachers to pose their questions at their convenience and have a response as early as after recess. This allows for the sharing of information at a much quicker pace than traditional communication, which can be a much longer process. One of our new teachers wrote, "I would get all these e-mails for all the new research and all the new information coming out. It was great!"

Spotlight on Anthony and Tan

Review the following e-mail communications between Anthony, a forty-something, second-career new teacher, and Tan, a thirty-three-year-old seasoned teacher.

Can you hear their unique voices in the e-mail exchanges?

Can you imagine the continued support that went on in the classroom?

Can you see the friendship and partnership that was forming?

Note: School or district e-mail communication in most public organizations is open to public access. Confidentiality may not be possible.

❖ ❖ ❖ ❖ ❖

From: Tan

To: Anthony

Sent: Wed 11/15/2006, 9:41 AM

Subject: Re: Lovely Visit

Anthony, I had a great time yesterday. I appreciate how gracious you were and how wonderful it was to go to another teacher's class and see so many great things being done. Please forward my thanks to Ms. C. because I enjoyed meeting her as well. In extension of our talks yesterday, here are the recommendations and ideas that we generated from our two meetings yesterday. Recommendations for Guided Reading:

1. Begin with a read aloud of a book on or above their reading level. I recommend chapter books as they give the students a continuous text to listen to daily. You can also add high vocabulary or rich tales for student interest.

2. Place information on charts from previous lessons or any skills you wish the students to retain or revisit.

3. Complete mini-lessons (10 to 15 minutes) on sounds daily rather than 25–30-minute phonics-based lesson.

4. Work one-on-one when needed after direct instruction for any student or students you feel need additional attention while remainder of group completes cooperative group or independent work.

5. Experiment with longer words after teaching phonics to see if students are able to chunk sounds (expansion of work). Give a word like irreversible—have students sound out the word, then come up with new words found using the letters inside, i.e., verse, is, believe, etc.

6. Allow students to read work independently and then record answers, and then share as a group.

7. Praise positive behavior from whole group to get student who may be off task back on task to try to emulate good behavior.

8. Create literary activities or use charts to have students work independently to follow along with you on the board.

9. Post classroom expectation of good behavior so that students will take responsibility for their areas, themselves, and group. (4 or 5 positive rules)

10. Extend activity, if time allows, for ideas presented in class. When you completed the very cool, cloze paragraph, have students retell story using their own new animal.

*** Post-it notes and index cards are great for activities listed above.

I hope these ideas can help and I will be calling you soon to arrange our face-to-face meeting, which has to be away from both our school sites in either November or December.

Thanks,
Tan

❖ ❖ ❖ ❖ ❖ ❖

From: Anthony
To: Tan
Sent: Tue 11/21/2006, 1:31 AM
Subject: Suggested Strategies That I Am Using

Hello Ms. M.,

I trust that all is well with you. I received your suggested strategies teaching in the classroom. I have begun reading to my guided reading group a chapter book. The book is titled A Series of Unfortunate Events. I read to them every day, ½ of a chapter. They seem to enjoy it. I have also challenged them at the end of class to create words from long words given to them on the board. They love this also. Did you know that there are 29 words that you can create from the word accommodation? I am sure there are more. Both of my classes

(Continued)

(Continued)

seem to enjoy this learning activity. Still hope to see you on December 7, 2006. What steps do I go through to get clearance from my principal? Do I need to get a form from somebody? Will talk to you later. A teacher at my school told me to tell you "Hi." Her name is Sheila. She said that she met you this past summer in the Summer workshops.

Until we see each other again.

Take Care,
Anthony

◈ ◈ ◈ ◈ ◈ ◈

From: Tan

To: Anthony

Sent: Tue 11/21/2006, 10:27 AM

Subject: Suggested Strategies That I Am Using

Attachments: Sub Coverage October–November 2006.pdf (16KB)

Hi, Anthony, ☺

My goodness, what were you doing up at 1 in the morning??? Working hard??

Please let Sheila know I said hello. She was in my session for our summer professional development in June. I had such a great time with her group.

A Series of Unfortunate Events is such a great book. One of the movies in the series is currently out for you to encourage the kids to see (w/Jim Carrey).

I am glad that you have taken some of the strategies we discussed and made them work in your class. Sometime in November or in December, we will need to meet for our Quarterly Face-to-Face (it has to be away from our workplaces). I wanted to know which date is good for you. In November or December. Maybe we could meet at Barnes and Nobles or Border's for coffee and conversations (as we call it at our school).

Also, please see the attached form for your principal to authorize regarding the day of our visit. You turn it in to your principal and/or school secretary and you are set. I am glad everything is going well. How are the twins?

Tan

Did you hear their unique voices? You can get a feel for the continued support that went on in the classroom. Were you able to see the friendship and partnership that was forming? Tan and Anthony kept up a strong partnership and the communication that occurred was a wonderful part of the personal and professional growth. The use of e-mail communication is typical of their generations—with both of them fitting into the Gen Xer category. Strong communication between the two partners helped Anthony transition into his new profession with more ease, and the bonds that formed were actually beneficial to both Anthony and Tan.

Using what we call mass e-mails can increase communication to a large group of new teachers. The benefits of using mass e-mails are many—the same message goes out to a large group of teachers; the systematic communication is helpful for teachers, just knowing someone is out there listening; the communication that occurs through the recurring e-mails opens the door for further communication. Web sites, blogs, and tweets are also useful avenues for dialogue.

Effective communication through the use of technology helps connect a diverse group of teachers by interwoven threads of similarities of the teaching profession. The trials and hardships, the joys and celebrations, all can be pulled into a conversation via e-mails, Web sites, blogs, tweets, or newsletters. It is another way to dialogue with a group of people. Good communication can cut across cultural divides and reach a diverse group of people.

An example of a mass communication e-mail that was sent out to approximately eighty-nine new teachers looked like this:

Dear Project GATE Mentees,

As you begin to plan your first school-site visit to your mentor's classroom, there is something I want you to think about prior to your visit.

At the heart of every effective teacher is the reflective teacher—the one who reflects about effective learning, teaching, while advancing your expertise and knowledge base.

Beaty (1997) maintains that "Reflective practice is important to the development of all professionals because it enables us to learn from experience. Although we all learn from experience, more and more experience does not guarantee more and more learning. 20 years of teaching may not equate to 20 years of learning about teaching but may be only one year repeated 20 times. There are many times when our normal reactions to events are insufficient themselves to encourage reflection. We should not rely solely on our natural process of reflecting on experience, but actively seek ways to ensure that reflection itself becomes a habit, ensuring our continuing development as a professional teacher in higher education" (p. 8). Reflecting on our own performance as teachers is one form of feedback.

As you take your journal to your mentor's classroom, consider how you can adapt what you saw/learned/loved to your own practice. What did you not like, as this too is reflective and learning. My first year teaching, I was paired up with the other special education teacher at my school whose organizational practices I simply thought were the best and she should be sharing with other teachers, but her teaching practices did not jive with my teaching styles. But I learned from her many things, but I also learned that there were things I wouldn't do.

So enjoy your visits, reflect, debrief at the end and feel free to ask, "Why did you do this or that?" I cannot wait to hear about your visits!

Let Dr. Gudwin or me know if there are any concerns regarding the visit, your mentor, or if there is anything else we can provide you with. If your mentor and you have not set up your first visit or there are concerns, please, please contact us. We want to make sure you receive the support that you need!!

Fondly,
Magda D. Salazar

Can you imagine what it feels like to be a new teacher in any type of community and to receive ongoing e-mails like the one above? Especially if it is from someone who clearly cares about your success, someone who gives you that guiding hand; it is like that old-fashioned letter arriving in the mailbox at just the right time. This is an excellent example of a component of communication that actually nurtures teachers in many different settings.

Table 5.4 is a self-assessment that may assist you in perfecting your intercultural communication. They are tips that we found very useful in working with educators.

Table 5.4 Self-Assessment: Tips for Intercultural Communication Success

Check Yes or No	Answer the Questions as Honestly as You Can	Reflection: Jot Down Your Thoughts
_____ Yes _____ No	Do I believe that my mentee has the desire to be the best he can be?	Reflection: How do I communicate that belief of my partner to him? _____ _____ _____ _____ _____
_____ Yes _____ No	Do I search for what Kee (2006, p. 1) refers to as "treasures of talent hidden below the surface of knowledge and skills" when I work with my new teacher?	Reflection: How do I communicate that belief of my partner to her? _____ _____ _____ _____ _____
_____ Yes _____ No	Do I bring out the best in my new teacher/partner and take him where he is to where he wants to be?	Reflection: How do I communicate that belief of my partner to him? _____ _____ _____ _____ _____
_____ Yes _____ No	I know that language, according to Kee (2006), is the second most important skill as a coach. "Language can build trust or bust the bank account!" (2006, p. 3). Do I build trust with my new teacher?	Reflection: How do I communicate that belief of my partner to her? _____ _____ _____ _____ _____
_____ Yes _____ No	I know that negative messages send an unconscious message to my mentee/partner.	Reflection: How do I ensure that negative messages are not part of my communication with my partner? _____ _____ _____ _____ _____

Check Yes or No	Answer the Questions as Honestly as You Can	Reflection: Jot Down Your Thoughts
_____ Yes _____ No	I know that the way in which I communicate messages to my mentee/partner makes a difference.	Reflection: How do I ensure that my communication reflects positive messages such as *In what ways is your discipline plan directly impacting your students' achievement?* instead of *Do you have a discipline plan in your classroom?* _____ _____ _____ _____ _____ _____ Reflection: How do I ensure that my communication reflects positive messages such as *What literacy strategies generate the most excitement for your students?* instead of *Have you been using the literacy strategies we talked/e-mailed about?* _____ _____ _____ _____ _____ _____

INTERCULTURAL COMMUNICATION AND THE STANDARDS OF THE PROFESSION

Many writers in the field of intercultural communication reassure us that intercultural competence can be acquired! For example, in a helpful handbook written for Illinois educators, Mangan (1995) reminded us, "Acquiring cultural knowledge and understanding is a lifelong process, built on a balance between formal study and direct experience. Professional competence for someone working in a multicultural classroom does not require an advanced degree in anthropology or sociology" (p. 7). We have direct experience in noticing how much teachers, veterans and new ones alike, enjoy developing their competencies. Those who have improved their intercultural communication competencies often realize that they are simultaneously demonstrating standards related to the teaching profession. As shown in Table 5.5, there are three sets of standards that many teachers apply to their own professional development activities: the Interstate New Teacher Assessment and Support Consortium (INTASC) (Council of Chief State School Officers, 2006) for beginning general educators, the Council for Exceptional Children (CEC) (2003) standards for beginning special educators, and the National Board Professional Teaching

Standards (NBPTS) (2006) for veteran teachers at all levels. By transferring the awareness level of individual differences to actual practice, teachers not only demonstrate the standards, but truly enhance both their teaching skills and their interpersonal skills at the same time. We have found that teachers who embrace cultural differences and who want to know more about them are those who can more effectively communicate with a diverse group of people.

Table 5.5 Professional Standards Related to Intercultural Communication Competence

Classroom Teachers INTASC (2006)	Special Educators CEC (2003)	Both (Veteran) Teachers NBPTS (2006)
Standard 3 requires teachers to understand *how learners differ.*	Knowledge and skills in understanding characteristics of learners with *different cognitive, physical, cultural, social, and emotional needs.*	Teachers adjust their practice according to *individual differences in their students.*

The unique communication patterns of teachers in urban school districts are reflective of the different populations that co-exist with each other. Communication by itself can be challenging, and an awareness of the multicultural and linguistic diversity that exists can enhance communication between teachers. Opening doors of communication through newsletters, e-mails, Web sites, blogs, tweets, personal dialogues, and, most important, reflective conversations is critical for the success of mentoring partnerships, which may positively affect the retention rate of new teachers. As we reflect upon our own embedded cultural traditions, we must pay attention to nonverbal communication, **intergenerational** communication, and written communication. Spending time reflecting on our own communication styles positively affects both our professional and our personal growth and enhances our interpersonal skills.

APPENDIX 5.1: PROJECT GATE NEWSLETTER

The following is a template for our Project GATE Newsletter, which you may want to use as a guide in developing your own avenues of communication.

Project GATE Gazette

Greetings from:
Denise and Magda...

Miami-Dade County Public Schools

Volume 1, Issue 7

May 2007

A warm hello to the Project GATE teams...

What an incredible year it has been and there are still 18 days left in this school year, so make them count! Thank you for sharing the wonderful FCAT Writing (for information on understanding the writing scores, please visit: http://fcat.fldoe.org) *and 3rd Grade Reading scores with us*—only an affirmation that you continue to shine and thrive in working with your students. Please feel free to email us and share with us the strides that your students have made this school year. We look forward to the celebration of these successes and many more at the Saturday, May 19, 2007 event.

As you begin to wrap up the school year, take the time to reflect on your teaching year: What worked? How can I make it better? What do I need to make it better? If there wasn't anything stopping me from making it better, what would I need? Let us know how we can help to make the closing of the school year a smooth transition for you.

If you have not heard the buzz, Summer HEAT sizzles! Summer HEAT is a wonderful five-day professional development opportunity. Check out the Summer HEAT Institutes/Academies offered during the weeks of June 11-15 & June 18-22, 2007.

All sessions are now up for previewing at the professional development website.

Don't procrastinate—courses will fill up in record time!

Special points of Interest:

- Websites of Interests
- Summer HEAT
- Literacy Strategies to Remember

Inside this issue:

"A teacher who is attempting to teach without inspiring the pupil with a desire to learn is hammering on cold iron." ~ Horace Mann

Project GATE : Getting Assistance for Teaching Effectively is a joint venture between Miami-Dade County Public Schools and Florida International University's Professional Development Partnership.

Miami-Dade County Public Schools
giving our students the world

Teaching is a Master Piece

Wall of Fame

Congratulations to
Project GATE Participants:

CEC Special Education School-site Teacher of the Year:
Kim Ferreira
Dr. Michale Krop Senior

CEC Special Education Teacher of the Year:
Maria Mesa
Miami Palmetto Senior

CEC Special Education Rookie School-site
Teachers of the Year:

Leslie Bienvenu
Greynolds Park Elementary

Maria Estevan
Gulfstream Elementary

Natalie Flores
Kendale Elementary

Cristina Ugalde
Miami Springs Senior

CEC Special Education Rookie Teacher of the Year:

Rafael Mendiola
Fienberg-Fisher Elementary

Wall of Fame

Congratulations to Project GATE Participants:

National Board Certified Teachers were honored on Saturday, February 17, 2007:

Aida Arocha, Kendale Lakes Elementary

Andriana Chaine, John Ferguson Senior

Raul Escarpio, Ben Sheppard Elementary

Kim B. Ferreira, Dr. Michael Krop Senior

Clidia K. Gonzalez, Eneida Hartner Elementary

Yesenia Marichal, Fienberg-Fisher Elementary

Maria Mesa, Miami Palmetto Senior

Jennifer L. Pepper, Killian Senior High

Education is the movement from darkness to light.
Alan Bloom

What's the Buzz around the State...

Center for Teaching Quality: Teacher-Authored Report on Performance Pay

In the first report of its kind, 18 expert teachers from across the nation have released a report proposing changes in the ways in which teachers have been compensated for years. Susan Bischoff, a fifth grade teacher at Ballard Elementary in Manatee County is one of the teachers credited with authoring the report. The group proposes radical changes to the traditional salary schedule and has made recommendations which, if implemented, could double, even triple, a teacher's income. To access the complete report as well as information about the Merit Award Program, visit http://www.fldoe.org/justforteachers.

Teacher Talk: An Inside Look at Florida Education: Show 3

Since the broadcast of the first show on the Florida Education Channel and the Florida Knowledge Network, districts across Florida have been placing the program into regular rotation on their local education channel, and teachers have been contacting me to have their school highlighted on the program. The show celebrates innovations made by Florida teachers, schools, and districts and features teacher interviews, student-produced segments, education news, and interesting stories about education in Florida. The third show, currently being broadcast, focuses on the following: Florida teacher survey results, Florida's online advising and academic planning system (FACTS.org) and the ePEP educational planner currently available in middle schools across Florida, as well as a student-produced interview with Marshall Skinner, director of Career and Technical Education programs in Martin County. Mr. Skinner discusses career academies, SUCCEED Florida! funding, and the variety of innovative programs available to students and teachers in Martin County. To access the Florida Education Channel and Florida Knowledge Network broadcast schedules for "Teacher Talk: An Inside Look at Florida Education" or to view programs online, visit http://www.fldoe.org/justforteachers. Be sure to check your local education channel for broadcast times in your area.

Florida Middle School Student Asking Spielberg to Remake The Diary of Anne Frank

Inspired by her sister, Stephanie Russo, the 2006 winner of Chancellor Yecke's "Middle School Summer Reading Book Challenge" administered by the Just Read, Florida! office, 7th grader Linda Russo decided to grab a good book and start reading. She chose, The Diary of Anne Frank and was so inspired by Anne's story, and the history of the Holocaust, that she decided to learn as much as she could about this period in history. She was led to the movie, produced in 1959, and decided that she would ask film director, Steven Spielberg, to remake the film to celebrate the 50th anniversary of the release of the original film. Linda is asking that Mr. Spielberg remake the film for release in 2009, and in her letter to the well-known director, she says "I am not Jewish, I am Catholic, but I think that is not what is important. Her diary shows that we are all the same and what happened to her and all the Jewish people in the Holocaust was very awful."

Source: Just for Teachers—http://www.fldoe.org/justforteachers/

Recognizing the Wealth that Parents Bring to Urban Schools
by Dr. Louie F. Rodríguez, Florida International University

Introductions

Earlier this year, a troubling story broke out of one of this nation's public schools. According to numerous media reports, a parent was called and demanded to come to school and pick up her disruptive child. During an apparently heated discussion with the teacher, some books were knocked on the floor whereby the teacher hit the panic button in her classroom. The parent and child proceeded to the office. There, the parent allegedly threatened the principal whereupon the police were called and the parent was arrested.

While the "facts" remain unclear, I immediately took a race and class analysis of the situation. I resorted to this analysis because the research shows that lower-class parents are more likely to be disregarded and treated indifferently by schools (Kozol, 1991). My hunch was that the parent was Black or Latina and probably of lower-class status while school officials (administrator and teacher) probably were not. I soon learned that the parent was Latina. However, what struck me even more than the incident itself was the public's outcry in response to it.

In today's age of the internet with immediate distribution and accessibility of information for anyone who has the means to do so, I began to search web blogs about the incident. Sure enough, in my estimation, about 95% of the public's outcry was laced with racist and classist responses about the mother and child. One person framed an opinion as a multiple choice question and it went something like this: "So, do you think the parent was: A) Cuban, B) Puerto Rican, or C) Dominican?" Other public opinions revolved around the "apple doesn't fall far from the tree" analogy, which implicated the mother's direct role in her child's "disruptiveness" and concentrated blame on the family. Across the numerous opinions that I read, there was little critique about the structural or cultural realities of schools and how those mediate the ways children and parents are treated, particularly those from historically marginalized communities of color. Aside from the blog opinions, many media stories reported that the parent needed a "timeout," a common term that parents or educators use to discipline children. The use of "timeout" to characterize the parent immediately infantilized this mother. This is particularly problematic when middle-class parents frequently advocate for the rights of their children and sometimes resort to threats such as a visit downtown. Yet, how many times are these parents characterized as needing a "timeout"? My guess is never.

Snapshot of the Research on Parent-School Dynamics

What is troubling about this situation and the ensuing public responses is the glaring normalization of the deficit-oriented perspectives that were used to characterize the mother and child. Deficit-oriented perspectives typically characterize communities of color as deficient often because of their cultural beliefs, parenting styles, language practices, and value systems (Valencia & Solorzano, 1997). Such deficit views typically clash with the white middle class norms and values of schools and since the cultures of these communities are different from that of schools and the people that work within them, communities of color are often characterized as deficient (Solorzano & Yosso, 2001). Research also shows that schools typically subtract the knowledge, experiences and expertise that communities of color bring (Ladson-Billings, 2000), often assuming that the knowledge is something that derives from textbooks and cannot possibly be drawn from the "funds of knowledge" of the people themselves—knowledge that is created by and with the school and community (Moll et al., 1992). Yet, not all educators harbor these views and there do exist examples of hope. The challenge to schools and the people within them is apparent and can be viewed in at least two ways--either capitalize on the strengths that parents bring and view schools as sources of encouragement, support, and hope, or perpetuate social inequality by harboring deficit-oriented perspectives and deny the need for parent engagement because it has always been that way (Noguera, 2001). I would like to focus on the former as a way to illuminate hope and argue the need for meaningful parent engagement, particularly in communities that have historically been neglected by larger society. In doing so, I will focus on two initiatives, outside of the Miami-area, to demonstrate what is possible.

Two Possibilities of Hope for Parent Engagement

Sharing a similar demographic profile to Miami, a multi-institutional partnership in Chicago between the State of Illinois, local public schools, community-based organizations, and local universities, created the Grow Your Own (GYO) Teachers Initiative. Contrary to the traditional parental involvement that revolves around attending parent conferences, an occasional fundraiser and sometimes workshops where educational experts tell parents what they need to be doing, the GYO Initiative targets parents, paraprofessionals, and other leaders in the community to become teachers and lead school-community collaboration. The GYO program believes in several core principles that shape their work with communities of color: 1) they bring assets that directly benefit schools, 2) they truly believe in the power of respectful relationships, 3) invest in school-community organizing to secure resources for parents, 4) provide the most neglected children with the best teachers, and 5) train highly competent classroom educators who can become teachers and community leaders. Outcomes show that GYO teachers are more likely to remain in critical shortage areas over time as opposed to teachers who come from the outside. The GYO initiative demonstrates what is possible when schools view and capitalize on the assets that parents bring to the school and wider community.

Recognizing the Wealth that Parents Bring to Urban Schools
by Dr. Louie F. Rodríguez, Florida International University

The second initiative has become a national program. The Parent School Partnership (PSP) Program is an effort born out of the Mexican American Legal and Defense Fund (MALDEF), an organization committed to protecting and enforcing the rights of Latinos across the nation. The PSP program believes in training parents, school-level personnel, and community-based citizens to take a leadership role in advocating for underserved children. Parents are taught about their rights and responsibilities, the structure and function of schools, how to navigate the parent/teacher conference, leadership development, and college access issues (The MALDEFian, 2007). In early 2007, a group of parents went to the California state legislature and advocated for a series of issues including financial aid for undocumented students, better communication to parents about college requirements, and support for parents of English Language Learners. The PSP Program models a direct challenge to any deficit perspectives of parents and communities and is committed to building true partnerships *with* parents for the purposes of advocating for an equitable education for all children. Both examples pose a challenge to educators to invest in the social, human, and cultural forms of capital that are salient within historically marginalized communities.

Critical Questioning

These examples pose a challenge to educators, particularly within systems that serve the most socially marginalized communities. Thus, a series of questions are worth posing, both for teachers and administrators, as an exercise to reflect on their individual and school-level practices. These questions revolve around the notion of community cultural wealth—that is, capitalizing on the strengths, assets, and skills that parents bring to the school (Yosso, 2005). That is, how have parents navigated these institutions in the past and what skills do they bring to the dialogue? What storytelling traditions do these communities bring and how can we legitimize these traditions, particularly as a way to get parents connected to schools? How can schools build a culture within them that values and invests in relationships with parents? What are the aspirations, hopes, and dreams of these communities? How can schools capitalize on the knowledge, experiences, and expertise of parents and use this as a pedagogical resource?

The opening situation that I discussed above is avoidable and should not be considered a normal occurrence in struggling schools. My belief is that until we get beyond deficit-notions of parents and communities and begin to recognize and invest in the wealth that parents bring to schools, educators will continue to struggle to engage parents with purpose, dignity, and justice. I close with a quote by Paulo Freire, Brazilian educator and philosopher:

"...the starting point for a political-pedagogical process must be precisely at the level of the people's aspirations and dreams, their understanding of reality and their forms of action and struggle" –Paulo Freire, *Learning to Question*

References

Grow Your Own Teachers Initiative. (2006). *Grow Your Own Teachers Initiative: Vision, Principles and Best Practices.* Grow Your Own Illinois. www.growyourownteachers.org

Kozol, J. (1991). *Savage inequalities.* New York, NY: Crown Books.

Ladson-Billings, G. (2000). Racialized discourses and ethnic epistemologies. In, N. Denzin & Y. Lincoln (Eds.), *Handbook of qualitative research,* (pp. 257-277). Thousand Oaks, CA: Sage Publications.

Moll, L. C., Amanti, C., Neff, D., & Gonzalez, N. (1992). Funds of knowledge for teaching: Using a qualitative approach to connect homes and classrooms. *Theory into Practice,* 31 (2), 132-141.

Noguera, P. A. (2001). Transforming urban schools through investments in social capital of parents. In S. Saegert, J. P. Thompson, & M. R. Warren (Eds.), *Social Capital and Poor Communities* (pp. 189-212).

The MALDEFian (2007). Empowering parents to advocate for their children. MALDEF Newsletter. April, 2007.

Solorzano, D., & Yosso, T. J. (2001). From racial stereotyping and deficit discourse toward a critical race theory in teacher education. *Multicultural Education,* 9 (1), 2-8.

Valencia, R., & Solorzano, D. (1997). Contemporary deficit thinking. In R. Valencia (Ed.), *The evolution of deficit thinking in educational thought and practice* (pp. 160-210). New York, NY: Falmer Press.

Yosso, T. J. (2005). Whose culture has capital? A critical race theory discussion of community cultural wealth. *Race Ethnicity and Education,* 8 (1), 69-91.

Teachers as Heroes, Dade Reading Council, Honors 2 GATE Teachers

On Saturday, April 28, 2007, two of our very own Project GATE teachers were recognized as Teachers as Heroes by Dade Reading Council. Magda was honored to be there supporting both of these stellar teachers.

Maria Estevan, Project GATE mentee at Gulfstream Elementary, was recognized for her innovative and caring way of working with her students with disabilities. She creatively infuses hands-on activities and literature into a picture perfect instructional lesson.

Tan Melton, Project GATE mentor at Kendale Elementary, was recognized for coaching her mentee, and many more during the 2006-2007 school year. She has not only impacted her students, but the students of teachers who have continuously visited her classroom as an "exemplary" inclusion classroom.

Literacy Strategies: Alternatives to Worksheets— Ideas From Our April Literacy PD by Dr. Gudwin

Hula Hoop Venn Diagrams

Venn diagrams are useful as a graphics organization tool when comparing two things (and particularly for use with younger children). Simple Venn diagrams are used, in which no more than two curves intersect at a common point. Shared characteristics are listed in the overlapping section allowing for easy identification of which characteristics are shared and which aren't. String or colored yarn can be used to make circles on the floor and manipulatives and pictures are strongly encouraged, or as demonstrated by Dr. Gudwin in April's Literacy Professional Development, Hula Hoops work wonderfully!

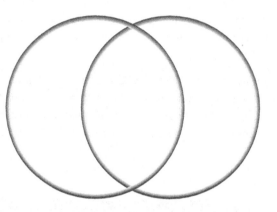

Sequencing Ladder

Most stories have a very definite sequence of events. Students gain a deeper understanding of the story by exploring this sequence. Use the Sequencing Ladder to help your students understand the concept of story development by analyzing events of the story (written, pictorial) and arranging them in logical sequential order. It can also be a "vocabulary ladder," a "retelling ladder," a "spelling ladder," and a "math ladder." Just use painters' tape... it will not harm the floor or carpeting.

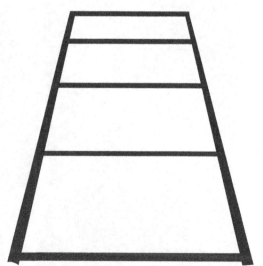

Miami-Dade County
Public Schools

Miami-Dade County Public Schools
giving our students the world

Mathematical Reasoning by Valerie Morris
Math Coach, Edison Senior High

Mathematical reasoning ability means thinking logically, being able to see similarities and differences in objects or problems, making choices based on those differences and thinking about relationships among things. You can encourage your child's mathematical reasoning ability by talking frequently with him about these thought processes.

Some Important Things Your Students Need to Know About Mathematics

You can help your students learn math by offering him/her insights into how to approach math. She will develop more confidence in her math ability if she understands the following points:

1. Problems can be solved in different ways.
2. Wrong answers sometimes can be useful.
3. Take risks!
4. Being able to complete mathematics in your head is important.
5. It's sometimes OK to use a calculator to solve mathematics problems.

Teacher Tools on the Internet

Teacher-Sites

Mathematic Interactive Websites

K-8 Website: www.aaamath.com

K-8 Website: www.aplusmath.com

K-6 Website: http://www.bbc.co.uk/skillswise/numbers/wholenumbers/

K-12 Website: www.coolmath.com

K-8 Website: www.funbrain.com

Secondary Website: http://highschoolace.com/ace/math.cfm

K-12 Website: http://illuminations.nctm.org/swr/index.asp

6

Mentoring in a Large Multicultural Urban District

Induction Programs and a Case Study

None of us got where we are solely by pulling ourselves up by our bootstraps. We got here because somebody—a parent, a teacher, an Ivy League crony, or a few nuns—bent down and helped us pick up our boots.

—Thurgood Marshall

As you read Chapter 6, we encourage you to reflect upon the following questions:

1. We want to revitalize our teacher induction program. What are the components that are critical for success?

2. What information can we gain from the case study? How can we replicate it in our district?

3. What information can we acquire from listening to new teachers?

To help you discover your own understandings of these questions, the content of the chapter is organized in the following sections: What Does the Research Say About Retention of Beginning Teachers? What an Induction Program Should Look Like, and a Case Study of one urban mentoring program for special education teachers. We anchor the content in the context of various scenarios that illustrate an effective teacher induction program.

Spotlight on New Teachers

Maria

Maria brought her bilingual Spanish heritage to her experiences as a new teacher in a predominately Hispanic and black, non-Hispanic elementary school in the southern section of a large urban school district. And yet she faced many obstacles. "From the beginning of the year, I was struggling." Her background is in psychology, and although she had little experience in working with children, she was hired at a school that historically had been underachieving and challenging. As a special education teacher who was placed in a varying exceptionalities classroom, she was responsible for serving students with various disabilities at the same time. Her physical body language indicates that she is quiet and shy; however, once she feels comfortable, Maria loves to talk about her experiences, and more importantly, the growth that occurred during her first year of teaching, a proud moment in her lifetime.

Janeth

Janeth is a beginning special educator for fourth, fifth, and sixth graders with mild disabilities. Although a teacher in her native country for eighteen years, this was her first year as a special educator in a predominantly black, non-Hispanic elementary school in the northern section of Miami, Florida. Her heavy Hispanic accent does not deter her from communicating with her students, but she does find it a challenge in communicating with her administrator.

Barbara

Barbara is not a new teacher. She began her teaching career working with children with emotional handicaps and was recently assigned to teach in a new exceptionality, a self-contained classroom of children with autism in the severe spectrum, in a predominately Hispanic and black, non-Hispanic elementary school in the southern section of the county, thus putting her in the category of new and early-career teachers. Although she has experience in teaching, she felt that the support of the mentoring program was essential.

Autism to me is most different from any other exceptionality in special education. The processing of the children, the behavior management is so different. I was put in there because I have an EH [emotional handicap] background; however, the behaviors are so different and the way you handle the behaviors is different. Totally different. And the neurological processing is totally different and the research is totally different. So, I wouldn't have handled it appropriately. . . . If I didn't have the mentoring program, I wouldn't have known where to go.

She felt like a new teacher again.

According to Stansbury and Zimmerman (2002), "a third of beginning teachers quit within their first three years on the job. . . . They ask the question, what lifelines can we offer so they will remain in the profession and develop into highly effective classroom educators?" (p. 1). Mentoring programs are critical for the success of new teachers (Salazar, Gudwin, &

Nevin, 2008). Brock and Grady (2006) acknowledge that the success of a mentoring program depends upon who initiates the induction program, who determines the size and scope of the program, and who is going to implement the program. Support programs can actually make a difference. Stansbury and Zimmerman (2002) focus on three aspects of support for new teachers:

1. Personal and emotional support, which is provided by experienced teachers who serve as listeners and sounding boards.

2. Task or problem-focused support, which is provided by experienced teachers who assist in problem solving.

3. Critical reflection on teaching practice, which is provided by experienced teachers who help the new teachers reflect on student achievement and personal teaching practices.

The above three components focus on the targeted support we know is needed in building an arena of support for new and early-career teachers.

WHAT DOES THE RESEARCH SAY ABOUT RETENTION OF BEGINNING TEACHERS?

Retention of beginning teachers and prevention of burnout continue to challenge school personnel. The foundation for the case study discussed later in this chapter is based on the concept of supply and demand. Policy and demographic factors have created a gap between the number of highly qualified teachers needed and the number available. This gap is filled with teachers who have not yet met state minimum qualifications to teach. One of the most challenging fields to staff is special education.

Educators new to the field face numerous challenges. At the core of national reform is the role of the teacher (Kliebard, 2004). In general, mentoring programs are critical for the success of new teachers, and a focused program dealing with specific issues such as the subgroup of special education can be beneficial. The significance of several factors (teacher qualifications, urban settings, presence of culturally and linguistically diverse populations, support for new teachers, and teacher leaders and mentors) that affect teacher attrition are described briefly.

Significance of Teacher Qualifications

After numerous school reforms, the constant consensus is that the quality of our schools depends on the quality of our teachers. According to Kozol (2005), "more experienced instructors teach the children of the privileged and the least experienced are sent to teach children of minorities" (p. 275). Schools with high percentages of poor and minority students often have less-experienced teachers than schools with students who are more affluent and white, even within the same school districts. Innovative efforts need to be established so that teacher preparation is better addressed. Additionally, intensive professional development must be designed so that teachers have the opportunity to increase their skills.

Significance of Urban Settings

Even in current times, with national attention on struggling schools, inequities persist in the placement of highly qualified teachers. All students, affluent or poor, high performing or low performing, minority or majority, need to have high-quality teachers. It is without a doubt that teacher retention in urban settings is a challenge. Newly hired teachers leave urban settings at higher rates than teachers in more affluent schools, from which departures are often attributed to job satisfaction. Research is clear about the characteristics of schools that teachers are most likely to leave (high-poverty schools, low-performing students), as well as policy recommendations for retaining teachers, such as implementation of induction programs.

Job satisfaction is a factor that affects teacher retention. Teachers are a hardworking group, sometimes putting in 50 or more hours a week; and about 15% of the teachers are working 60 hours or even more (National Education Association, 2003). The supply-and-demand gap widens for certain fields within education, such as special needs and English language learners (ELL) in urban settings. Of those who left the field of teaching, 32% resulted from job dissatisfaction, according to Luekens, Lyter, and Fox (2004).

> My first year was much tougher than I expected. I had no curriculum, no support, no experienced special education teacher in the building, and no real experience at the district level. I was at school almost every day until 6 or 7 o'clock. I would arrive before the sun came up and leave after dark. By November I called my mom one night just bawling on the phone to tell her I wanted to work at Belks or Winn Dixie—I didn't care. I was not going back to teach!
>
> —Jessica (quoted in Whitaker, 2000, p. 28)

If Jessica had had a mentor who guided her along the way during those beginning times, would she have had more of a successful year? If there was an effective teacher induction program in her district, would that have provided Jessica the tools she needed? Absolutely!

Significance of Culturally and Linguistically Diverse Populations

Struggling students and English language learners are more likely to have teachers who are not adequately prepared to teach them. These challenges demand renewed attention and action and are the primary focus of our case study. In a large urban district, there is often a culturally and linguistically diverse population, which adds to the database of knowledge that new teachers must acquire. Nationally, over 4.1 million students (8.5%) are English language learners (Paige, 2004); however, in the following case study, the ELL population is 52.5%. This district has the largest minority student population in the state and is the only district in Florida where there are more minority teachers than white, non-Hispanic teachers (Florida Department of Education, 2007). In Miami, Florida, the overall student population is composed of 9.6% white, non-Hispanic; 27.6% black, non-Hispanic; 60.4% Hispanic; and 2.4% other. According to Miami-Dade County Public Schools, the top ten languages spoken in this district are Spanish, Haitian Creole, French, Portuguese, Zhongwen (Chinese), Arabic, Russian, Urdu, Hebrew, and Vietnamese (2006a). Teachers face many challenges in teaching, but add to those the culturally and linguistically diverse factors, and the challenges can be overwhelming to a beginning teacher, especially when dealing with the barrier of communication of both students and parents, and even peer teachers and colleagues.

Significance of Support for New Special Education Teachers

Teachers of students with disabilities must be proficient in legal and compliance issues in addition to curriculum and instructional practices. As this population is now receiving more and more instruction in general education classrooms, special educators must have an increased knowledge about the general education curriculum, and general educators must have an increased knowledge of learners who are diverse in various ways. Added to the increased diversity of the students attending school, one of the challenges is the lack of diversity in the current generation of teachers nationwide.

Pugach (2005) revealed that little research has been conducted on the program effects of preparing potential teachers to work with students with disabilities. We know that well-prepared teachers stay in the field longer and also produce higher student achievement (National Council for Accreditation of Teacher Education, 2006); however, retention of beginning special education teachers and prevention of burnout continue to challenge school personnel.

Significance of Teacher Leaders as Mentors

Killion and Harrison (2005) describe mentor teacher leaders as those who facilitate learning, model, demonstrate lessons, co-plan, co-teach, and provide feedback, while building and maintaining a trusting relationship. When coupled with coaching, teacher leaders can help new teachers see their teaching world through a different lens as suggested by McNeil and Klink (2004). Specifically, new teachers are encouraged to achieve their goals through interaction within a positive, collegial relationship (Brock & Grady, 2007). When a new teacher has a mentor who will "be there" to support and assist, who will be that guide and friend, the chance for success is increased.

An exemplary mentor teacher leader should have a deep understanding of teaching and learning and should be a passionate teacher and learner too. As Robbins (2004) so eloquently states, "We know now that teacher quality is the factor that matters most for student learning. We must be diligent in making plans for mentoring. Precious resources are at stake" (p. 161). The increase of student achievement is ultimately the goal of providing avenues of success for a new teacher. Connect these thoughts to the following repeated scenario of Raul Escarpio, which is included also in Chapter 3:

> Being a mentor has allowed me to further reflect on my practice in my classroom. As a mentor, Project GATE allows me to hone in on my abilities and think "outside the box" in terms of culturally and linguistically diverse learners. I know that I need to be the kind of teacher that goes that extra mile because that is what I instill in my mentee and want her to learn. It is not about the most creative lesson or the most colorful bulletin boards that will make me a better teacher; it is about caring enough about my students that allows me to be the best professional that I can be. I try to see the mentee as an extension of myself in the field and try to assist her the way I would have wanted to be assisted. It is refreshing to see that she has taken the lead and become independent in her practice. She trusts her instincts and values her creativity. While I would like to think that her growth was a direct result of my actions, I know better. She always had that gift, that sparkle, that light: She just needed the encouragement and validation. If this program provides that confidence and leads to greater retention in the field, then this program has been a blessing. Some would say that our students are our greatest treasure (and deservedly so), but in looking at beginning teachers, they are also our treasure. Without their enthusiasm and passion for students, then education just becomes mechanical and boring. I wish I would have had this program when I began teaching.
>
> —Raul Escarpio

Raul has that deep understanding of teaching and learning and is a passionate teacher and learner too.

WHAT AN INDUCTION PROGRAM SHOULD LOOK LIKE

What Is a Teacher Induction Program?

A teacher induction program provides systematic structure of support for beginning teachers or teachers new to the district and involves those support systems used to assist them in becoming competent and effective professionals in the classroom. Induction programs also help develop an understanding of the local school and community cultures. We recommend that well-developed teacher induction programs consist of the following components:

- **New Teacher Orientation:** New teacher orientation begins the comprehensive induction program by providing a formal orientation to learn key information about the district, curriculum, and school. It includes, but is not limited to, the district reading program, information regarding the state standards, classroom management, district procedures, and orientation to the school climate.

- **Mentoring Partnerships:** Mentoring partnerships provide the beginning teacher with an opportunity to work closely with and learn from an experienced mentor teacher leader. The mentoring partnership is shaped by the activities in which the beginning teacher and mentor participate together. Setting aside structured time is a necessary part of the mentoring relationship as it enables mentoring activities such as observation, co-teaching, and lesson planning to take place. Time and commitment within the team are critical, and administrators are encouraged to pair mentors with new and early-career teachers by grade level, content area, or teaching assignment.

- **Professional Learning Communities:** The purpose of professional learning communities is to link the beginning teachers with a network of experienced teachers, in addition to their mentors, a network on which they can rely for assistance and guidance while participating in high-quality professional development opportunities provided over time.

- **Professional Development for Beginning and Early-Career Teachers:** Beginning teachers need professional development opportunities that are specifically designed for the beginning teacher. This professional development provides the beginning teacher with critical information, such as curriculum, lesson planning, district-mandated requirements, and other topics that are relevant to them during their first year in the classroom. A needs assessment survey is beneficial in tailoring the professional development directly to their needs.

- **Professional Development for Mentors:** Mentors need to receive training in the skills of effective coaching, as well as opportunities to meet with other mentors to share successes and troubleshooting strategies. These opportunities are an important part of the mentor's professional development and can also take the form of learning communities.

In Table 6.1, we have listed our recommendations for the preplanning induction committee to include a minimum of the roles listed.

Table 6.1   Who Should Be Included in Developing an Induction Plan?

✓	*Who?*
	Veteran teachers, with representatives of all curriculum, special education, bilingual, and special areas
	New and early-career teachers, with representatives of all curriculum, special education, bilingual, and special areas
	Principals
	Central office staff
	University staff
	Union representation

Why Do Beginning Teachers Have Difficulty?

- **Beginning teachers are often idealistic and have unrealistic expectations:** They may have a pedagogical idea of what their job should be like; they often wear rose-colored glasses at the start of their career. *Bernard thought that teaching was the perfect job, that it would be an easy one after completing his college degree.*

- **Beginning teachers may experience crisis and challenges:** Some challenges include a disgruntled parent, a legal hearing, or dealing with complex certification requirements. *Magda was in her first year teaching when she was slammed with a high-profile case initiated by the district's most feared student advocate. Because of her mentor's strong support, as well as a team of district and region staff who were truly there for her every step of the way, Magda not only survived the very stressful month-long drama, but also excelled as an educator, building the blocks of confidence and competence to form a firm foundation of her career.*

- **Beginning teachers think they should know better:** Beginning teachers are reluctant to seek help because after a four-year college degree, they think they should know and be prepared. *Rosie didn't feel comfortable asking for help. She felt that she was already supposed to know what she was doing.*

- **Beginning teachers receive little or inadequate support:** According to Billingsley (2005), 60% of new special education teachers participated in formal mentoring programs, but one-third of them did not find it useful. *Anika rarely sees her mentor, who appears overwhelmed herself. Anika doesn't feel like she has anyone to turn to.*

We believe that high-quality induction programs are needed, regardless of how well new teachers are prepared. All teachers need some form of support and assistance. Many struggle with how to apply the acquired knowledge or have difficulty applying it in their particular situation.

- Half of all new special education teachers leave during the first five years (Billingsley, 2005).
- According to Ingersoll (2001), teacher turnover is 13.2% within the first two years.

Induction Goals and Planning

Induction programs do more than focus on survival needs. They provide professional development opportunities, pedagogical guidance, and ongoing support beyond the first year of teaching. According to Billingsley (2005), the following should be the goals of an induction program:

- Improve student achievement
- Promote the well-being of teachers and reduce the isolation and stress that many teachers experience
- Transmit the culture of the school and school system to new teachers
- Increase teacher retention

A CASE STUDY

Miami-Dade County Public Schools is the fourth largest school system in the nation. This district sponsors numerous successful comprehensive teacher induction programs, one of which was Project GATE, a systematic structure of support for new and early-career special education teachers to assist them in becoming competent and effective professionals. Brock and Grady (2007) suggest that such programs expect multiple outcomes such as retention of qualified teachers and enhanced professional growth.

Project GATE (Getting Assistance for Teaching Effectively) focused on mentor teacher leader partnerships and professional development for both mentor teacher leaders and new and early-career special education teachers.

In 2001–2002, Project GATE was developed by the district's Division of Special Education, in collaboration with Florida International University, and started off with fifteen mentoring teams, consisting of a beginning special education teacher and a mentor teacher leader. It grew to twenty-five mentoring teams in 2002–2003, thirty-two teams in 2003–2004, forty-three teams in 2004–2005, and forty-four teams in 2005–2006. There was an extensive increase to eighty-nine teams in 2006–2007, due to an expansion of the program with additional support from the district's Office of Professional Development. The data of this chapter focus on the experiences during the 2006–2007 school year when we became directly involved with Project GATE, continuing the collaboration with Florida International University. We interviewed each potential mentor teacher leader, following the predetermined criteria and interview questions shared in Table 6.2. The mentor teacher leaders were awarded a $1,000 stipend for their successful involvement in the program, thanks to the collaborative efforts of Florida International University and Miami-Dade County Public Schools. The mentors were then matched up one-to-one to a participating new or early-career teacher. An evaluation conducted at the end of the 2006–2007 school year indicated that 97% of the new teachers attributed their success to Project GATE.

Table 6.2 Mentor Criteria and Interview Questions

✓	Criteria
	Three years or more of successful classroom teaching experience
	Recommendation of school-site administrator
	Certified in a specific area (to be matched up with new teacher)
	Completed Clinical Education Training or another mentor training program
	(Optional) National Board Certified Teacher
✓	Face-to-Face Interview Questions
	What is the most important component in making a lesson effective for all learners?
	What are some effective management strategies you've implemented in your own classroom?
	What do you think makes for a good mentoring program?
	How would you handle a mentee who is not receptive to suggestions?
	What makes you a good mentor?

Objective of Project GATE

The Project GATE objective was to implement a mentoring program for eighty-nine newly hired special education teachers (including those who were out-of-field and those within their first three years of teaching) and to improve job success and satisfaction as well as position retention. Newly hired teachers who were teaching in low-performing schools were given priority and were recruited for participation in the mentorship program. This was an optional, voluntary subgroup of the district's existing new teacher program.

Requirements of Project GATE Participants

Mentoring Classroom Visits: A total of five site visits occurred, with three visits to be completed by the mentor visiting the beginning teacher's classroom, and two visits by the beginning teacher to the mentor's classroom. Each of these visits was followed up by debriefing of the observations, with ongoing discussions of best practices in special education encouraged.

Face-to-Face Collaborative Time: Mentors and beginning teachers scheduled a minimum of ten hours for face-to-face collaboration time outside of the classroom. At these meetings, they discussed issues related to previous classroom observations, as well as classroom questions and concerns that had developed. This outside meeting also encouraged rapport and trust building in the partnership.

Web-Based or Phone Collaborative Time: Mentors and beginning teachers engaged in Web-based or phone mentoring time. E-mails and phone conversations were used to address classroom questions and concerns.

Where Did the Case Study Take Place?

Miami, Florida, is often referred to as the capital of Latin America. It has long welcomed people from around the world and particularly those from Latin America. Its huge urban school district of culturally and linguistically diverse classrooms makes up the fourth largest school system in the nation.

According to the Office of Professional Development's *Mentoring and Induction for New Teachers* (Miami-Dade County Public Schools [M-DCPS], n.d.), the district "anticipates that 8,000 new teachers will be by hired by 2010. . . . The teacher turnover rate in M-DCPS for the 2005–2006 school year was 4.65%" (p. 2).

Studies indicate that as many as 20% of new teachers leave the teaching field after only three years and close to 30% after five years (Blazer, 2006). Comparatively, in the state of Florida, 11% of new graduates who taught in Florida public schools left the classroom after one year (Florida Department of Education, 2003). In contrast, in 2005, 17.3% of the teachers were new to Miami-Dade County Public Schools (M-DCPS, 2006a); however, the teacher turnover rate in 2005–2006 was 4.65% (M-DCPS, 2006b).

Participants

During the 2006–2007 school year, Miami-Dade County Public Schools employed over 20,000 teachers, of whom 21% were special education teachers serving over 68,000 students with disabilities. The selected participants of this case study were new or early-career special education teachers who participated in Project GATE during the 2006–2007 school year. Appendix 6.2 includes the interview questions provided to the participants, and Appendix 6.3 includes the beginning teacher requirements. Applications used are shared in Appendix 6.4 and Appendix 6.5.

Data Sources

We used the method of purposeful sampling (Bogdan & Bilken, 2007) of teachers who had completed Project GATE during the 2006–2007 school year. The participants were selected because they were employed in schools of low social economic status that were considered hard to staff. Teachers were interviewed in order to "understand [their] experiences and reconstruct events in which [we] did not participate" (Rubin & Rubin, 2005, p. 3). After signing consent documents, which had been approved by the institutional review boards of both the university and the school district, the interviews were conducted with new and early-career special education teachers in the district to capture their perspectives. The interview questions (Appendix 6.1) contained relatively open-ended questions, but were focused on eliciting participants' perceptions of the mentoring program.

From the interview data, themes were first drawn out from the questions. The concepts and themes were then compared among participants (Rubin & Rubin, 2005). Then themes that were most important for understanding factors that contributed to the retention of special education teachers were identified. The five major themes identified from the voices of beginning teachers are discussed in the section later in this chapter, What Did We Discover?

Figure 6.1 shows the results, indicating the responses of the participants through graphic information using a sampling of four of the interview questions:

- Which of the following best describes your current position?
- What grade levels(s) do you currently teach or are you assigned to?
- When did you participate in Project GATE?
- Do you see yourself remaining in your current position for the upcoming school year?

Based on a needs assessment, the beginning teachers participated in six days of professional development sessions consisting of instructional and behavioral strategies, compliance, and procedures regarding district mandates. Teachers participated in face-to-face collaborative meetings, as well as classroom walk-throughs with feedback. The following is indicative of the feedback provided via an online survey:

How satisfied are you with the following, as they pertain to Project GATE?	
Length of a mentoring program	98% satisfied
Frequency of face-to-face collaboration	96% satisfied
Location of face-to-face collaboration	96% satisfied
Knowledge, expertise of your mentor	100% satisfied
The mentor's support, openness, and acceptance of you as a new teacher	96% satisfied
The accessibility of your mentor	96% satisfied
How well your own needs were addressed by the mentoring program	98% satisfied
Please respond to the following questions solely as they pertain to Project GATE:	
The mentoring experience was beneficial to my professional experience.	96% agree
The knowledge and skills acquired through the mentoring experiences were relevant to improve student performance.	98% agree
The mentoring process helped me to become a better teacher.	96% agree
The mentoring process was an important component of my professional development.	96% agree

Figure 6.1 Four Sample New- and Early-Career Interview Questions

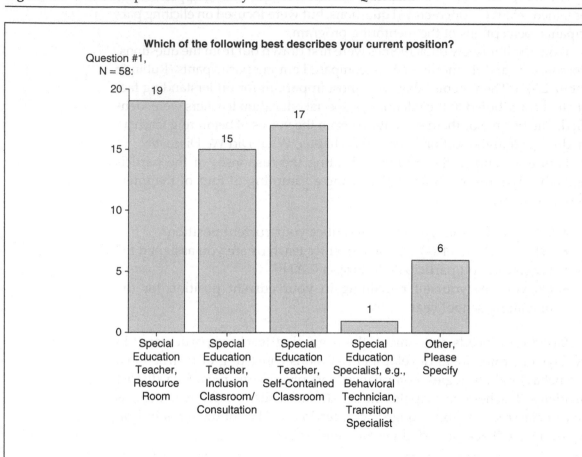

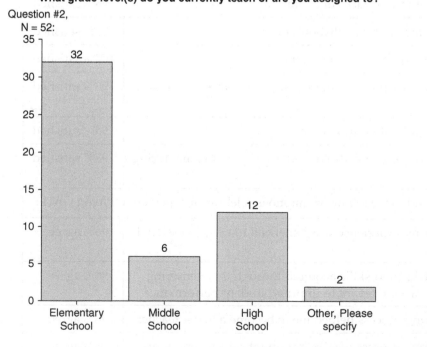

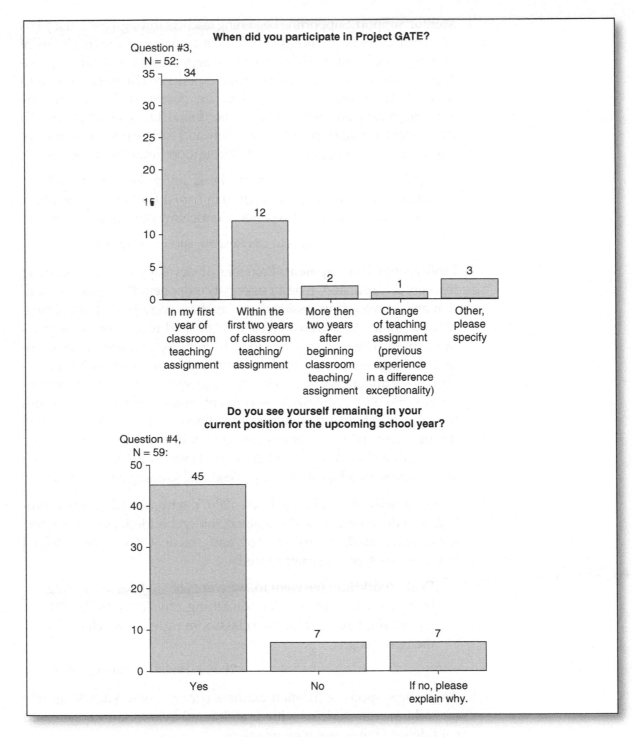

When did you participate in Project GATE?

Question #3, N = 52:

(bar chart)
- In my first year of classroom teaching/assignment: 34
- Within the first two years of classroom teaching/assignment: 12
- More then two years after beginning classroom teaching/assignment: 2
- Change of teaching assignment (previous experience in a difference exceptionality): 1
- Other, please specify: 3

Do you see yourself remaining in your current position for the upcoming school year?

Question #4, N = 59:

(bar chart)
- Yes: 45
- No: 7
- If no, please explain why.: 7

Furthermore, the data indicated that 100% of the participants indicated that each new teacher should have a mentor and 92% indicated that Project GATE made a huge difference in their teaching as a beginning teacher.

What Did We Discover?

We identified five major themes from the interviews: (1) support, (2) professional development, (3) sense of belonging, (4) communication, and (5) personal growth. In addition to representative verbatim quotes from participants, each theme is discussed in relation to extensive research on mentoring special education teachers.

1. **Mentor Support.** Supporting beginning teachers through their first years of teaching can be challenging as new teachers go through phases of development. Mentor teacher leaders must wear different hats depending on the phases of development being experienced by their team members. Often, mentor teacher leaders are described as wearing the following hats: guide, role model, listener, friend, lifesaver, and so on. We have included many scenarios from new and early-career teachers representing the positive impact of mentor support throughout this book.

> Maria is not only my mentor, she is my guide and friend. Although she is much younger than I am, I find that her great professional skills and experience enrich my day-to-day work.
>
> —Janeth Del Rosario, special education teacher

2. **Professional Development.** Professional development for beginning teachers is considered to be an essential component that leads to retention and increased professionalism. Teachers were provided information on topics that were relevant to them during their first years in teaching. The program provided learning opportunities via intensive, small-group professional development sessions on such topics as effective reading practices, learning strategies and accommodations permissible on the statewide assessment, and compliance procedures for special education requirements. These topics were identified through a needs assessment as critical in addressing the needs of new special education teachers, and the sessions varied in format, including large groups, small groups, and professional learning communities.

The comment of Fogarty and Pete (2007), who regard effective professional development as "sustained, job-embedded, collegial, interactive, integrated, results oriented, and practical" (p. 41), is reflected in what a first-year teacher shared:

> Every workshop we went to, we were able to take something back. We were able to take something physically back with us and implement it into the classroom right away. That was the best thing.
>
> —Maria, special education teacher

As the new special education teachers became more knowledgeable in working with students with disabilities, they also saw an increased confidence in their teaching practices.

> I was able to go to many workshops that dealt with the various aspects of my profession, including Individual Educational Plan preparation and planning, inclusion classes, reading ideas and reading programs, planning and intervention strategies, and behavior interventions. . . . Through Project GATE, I was able to begin a development program for myself and be more aware of my responsibility as a professional and instill those ideas at my school site.
>
> —Barbara Essinger, special education teacher

3. **Sense of Belonging.** Support to new teachers has been shown to be critical to teacher retention, particularly from colleagues. One way of providing support to teachers is through collaborative environments at the school site, and this has proven to be beneficial to preventing burnout (Billingsley, 2005). Teachers who have a network of support develop a sense of belonging, which is one of the more basic needs in Maslow's Hierarchy of Needs. The sense of belonging is corroborated by this teacher's response:

> It gave me the structure I was looking for. It gave me the guidance I was looking for. I didn't feel so lonely. I didn't feel like a little fish in a big ocean with nowhere to go. I felt more like it was a pool of fish. I felt like it was a community. I felt a sense of belonging. It feels like a SPED community, or I don't know if it was because we were all special education teachers, but it felt more like a family, not like I was a stranger. It made a huge difference in my first year teaching.
>
> —Maria Estevan, special education teacher

4. **Communication.** Communication is paramount and is the heart of mentoring. Special education teachers often feel isolated; however, communicating with other special education teachers can "assist in the development of collegiality and collaboration among those who are too often left out of the day-to-day communication and support network" (Boyer & Gillespie, 2003, p. 1.7). Communication, such as e-mail or face-to-face, is critical to the success of new teachers (Pitton, 2006). "Constructivist teachers are not isolated from their peers, instead, they appear to play an active role, particularly when colleagues are discussing issues related to content and pedagogy" (Judson & Lawson, 2007, p. 490). Communication can be critical to development as a teacher:

> I would get all these e-mails for all the new research and all the new information coming out. . . . Mary [mentor] would offer advice and constructive ideas in such a way that you would not take it as criticism and I am a very, very sensitive person. And she was always sharing.
>
> —Barbara Essinger, special education teacher

5. **Personal Growth.** To become empowered, teachers must understand their place in the educational arena. New teachers not only face challenges professionally, but they also feel personal challenges. Supporting new teachers should encompass support for their personal growth as well. Opening these doors may not only improve teacher quality, but also improve their self-worth.

> I have grown so much, both as a person and as a professional. I have more confidence personally. I take risks, and feel competent in my judgment. I have learned to take care of myself better, even by eating well and finding time for

exercise. Having a newfound contentment in my work has renewed my personal growth and well-being.

—Anonymous

6. **Additional Support.** Appendix 6.6 includes a sample Yearly Calendar/At-A-Glance, one of the avenues that we used to communicate our annual plan with the new teachers and their mentors. It helps when everyone is on the same page! One of the most positive additional aspects of this program was the sincere support from the district staff. A true sense of caring and desire for teacher success were evident throughout the program. In replicating this mentoring program, there must be support from a core of educators spearheading the project, with a similar desire for teacher success and the giving of one's own mentoring experiences with both heart and knowledge shared unselfishly.

> The communication and planning for the workshops and events that they felt we might be interested in was the most beneficial from district support. These women, Ms. Salazar and Dr. Gudwin [central office staff], are an incredible team who really know what new teachers need to be successful.
>
> —Leslie Bienvenu, elementary inclusion teacher

> The central office support staff provided everything: . . . planning, sessions, knowledge, understanding, support, professionalism, and advice.
>
> —Anthony Symons, elementary
> general education inclusion teacher

From the Voices of the Participants

FROM THE VOICES OF A DIVERSE GROUP OF NEW AND EARLY-CAREER TEACHERS PARTICIPATING IN PROJECT GATE: A MENTORING PROGRAM FOR NEW SPECIAL EDUCATION TEACHERS

This program provides mentoring activities to improve the quality of skills and knowledge of beginning teachers. My mentor, Dayana Cadaya, is an excellent professional who provided me with a strong support. I liked the opportunity to observe the classrooms and strategies of another mentor to gather more and different ideas. Learning from the diversity of different mentors is the best way to teach the diverse students that I face in the classroom.

—Rafael Mendiola, elementary resource
special education teacher, second career

Meeting with my mentor for face-to-face meetings at coffee shops, which allowed for practical and less stressful conversations, was one of the mentoring activities I liked the most.

—Karol Pena, elementary resource special education teacher

Central Office Support

It is easier to say what I didn't find helpful, because everything was helpful—the list is long! I sent out an SOS signal and they responded right away. Magda came out to my classroom and even took me to other schools to see other effective teachers in practice. Dr. Gudwin is a beacon of positive energy. She encouraged and inspired me to become more involved in the Special Education communities. I am a better, more well-rounded teacher because of their support. . . . Magda, thank you for keeping me in mind. It's amazing that with all you do you can still remember little old me. I really feel the love. (And I'm not kidding.) I still have some rough days when I question, Why am I doing this? And then there are the good days, when an obstinate student actually does his work without being told, or when a student who can't read well smiles after reading a few sentences. It is all worth it. Thank you both.

—Maria Estevan, elementary resource special education teacher

I will always remember that Ms. Salazar went so far as to pick me up all the way from Little Havana just so I can attend a training. That is dedication! [Ms. Salazar, who lived three blocks from the professional development training site, volunteered to drive 44 miles roundtrip to ensure Iliana was able to attend the workshop.]

—Iliana Valdez, elementary inclusion teacher

The positive feedback when Dr. Gudwin and Magda came out to visit and the immediate responses to my concerns of teaching was so beneficial to me.

—Olivia Mulet, elementary resource special education teacher

Professional Development

Saturday's workshop was energizing and affirming for me. I enjoy sharing ideas with my colleagues as well as receiving new and practical information to improve my teaching. When I heard Raul [a mentor] and Magda, it gave me a sense of relief that I was already doing some things as I should. I received many new ideas, for example, Raul presented many good ideas for centers and ways to motivate the students. Magda had us participate in a group activity where we had to Jigsaw a section of the accommodations book in order to have a better understanding of the content and how to apply it in the classroom and while administering our statewide test. Raul also modeled a behavior management technique with a rain stick to help the students focus on the task at hand. . . . Thank you Magda, Raul, and Denise, for helping me become a better teacher for my kiddos!

—Soraya Fumero, elementary inclusion teacher

I attended quite a few professional developments offered by Project GATE and our District, such as CRISS training [Project CRISS: Creating Independence Through Student-Owned Strategies], Conscience Discipline, Education Summit, and Dr. Asa Hillard's presentation. Thank you for the opportunities! I learned so much that helped me in my classroom.

—Mildred Boveda, elementary inclusion teacher

Sense of Belonging

Project GATE allowed me to connect and make friends with other first-year teachers that were going through the same experiences that I was. They have been a great support for me.

—Rachel Johnson, elementary self-contained special education teacher

(Continued)

(Continued)

I am part of a group who cares. I have met many people in the field, thanks to Project GATE, who I can turn to when I need help.

—Cristina Ugalde, secondary self-contained special education teacher

Communication

I am truly grateful to Project GATE for the support and communication I have received this year. You have had a very positive impact on much of what I have done and experienced as a new teacher. I just want to say "thank you" for including me in the Project GATE program—it is a phenomenal success! By the way, I am deeply moved by the movie you sent—still wiping tears from my eyes—and I cannot wait to get back to my students after the winter break.

—Leslie Bienvenu, elementary inclusion teacher

Personal Growth

I have grown so much this year, both personally and professionally. I learned that I can stand on my own two feet and that I am indeed a teacher. And I know I will become an even more effective teacher as the years go by. I am now able to tackle a problem and believe in my decision. Thank you Project GATE for guiding me along like a beacon of light.

—Megan Dennie, elementary resource teacher

Listening to the voices of new teachers keeps us focused on what mentoring programs should offer. We have much to learn from our teachers, as case studies can show us.

Recommendations

Partnering a beginning teacher with an effective mentor teacher leader can have profound effects on the success of the teacher. New and early-career teachers can learn to be more effective teachers if we give them the right tools and ongoing support. From these experiences and the review of current literature, we know that well-prepared new teachers stay in the field longer and produce higher student achievement (National Council for Accreditation of Teacher Education, 2006). With the effective mentoring components, new teachers, whether special education or general education, can be taken to new heights of teaching—the levels of impact are quite evident, levels that can be quantifiable for any teacher.

Overall, the results indicate that the participants of the mentoring program believed that they were provided support in a variety of effective ways. Support was based upon their individual needs and communication of their needs with school district administrators. In addition, there were similar threads of needs and support systems that were viewed as effective by the teachers. It was evident to us and to the participants that a quality mentoring partnership can indeed make a positive impact on the teaching lives of new and early-career teachers, thus enhancing the achievement of their students.

APPENDIX 6.1: BEGINNING TEACHER QUESTIONNAIRE

1. Please list your name and school name and school address (demographic regarding school location):
   a. Name:
   b. School:
   c. School address:
   d. Mail code:
   e. City:
   f. State:
   g. Zip code:
   h. E-mail address:
   i. Ethnicity:

2. Which of the following best describes your current position?
   ☐ Special education teacher—resource room
   ☐ Special education teacher—inclusion classroom/consultation
   ☐ Special education teacher—self-contained teacher
   ☐ Special education specialist, e.g., behavioral technician, program specialist

3. What grade level(s) do you currently teach or are you assigned to?
   ☐ Elementary school
   ☐ Middle school
   ☐ High school

4. When did you participate in the mentoring program?
   ☐ In my first year of classroom teaching or assignment
   ☐ Within the first two years of classroom teaching or assignment
   ☐ More than two years after beginning classroom teaching or assignment
   ☐ Change of teaching assignment (previous experience in a different exceptionality)
   ☐ Other, please specify:

5. Do you see yourself remaining in your current position for the upcoming school year?
   ☐ Yes
   ☐ No. If no, please explain why:

6. Do you see yourself in a teaching position for the next five years?
   ☐ Yes
   ☐ No. If no, please explain why:

7. Would you recommend the mentoring program to a new teacher? Please explain.
   ☐ Yes
   ☐ No. If no, please explain why:

8. Please list the mentoring activity you liked most.

9. What was the least valuable part of the mentoring experience?

10. In your opinion, what could be done to improve the mentoring program?

11. How satisfied are you with the following:

1 = Very dissatisfied; 2 = Dissatisfied; 3 = Somewhat satisfied; 4 = Satisfied; 5 = Very satisfied

Length of mentoring program

    1   2   3   4   5

Frequency of face-to-face collaboration

    1   2   3   4   5

Location of face-to-face collaboration

    1   2   3   4   5

Knowledge, expertise of the mentor

    1   2   3   4   5

The mentor's support, openness, and acceptance of you as a beginning teacher

    1   2   3   4   5

The accessibility of the mentor(s), i.e., if you needed assistance or had questions and needed to get a hold of the mentor

    1   2   3   4   5

The responsiveness of the mentor(s) to your requests for help or assistance with questions or concerns

    1   2   3   4   5

The quality of the mentor's follow-up responses, support, or assistance provided to you when you made the request

    1   2   3   4   5

The organization and clarity of the materials you received as a participant in the mentoring program

    1   2   3   4   5

The usefulness of the content or topics that were covered during professional development

    1   2   3   4   5

How well your own needs were addressed by the mentoring program

1   2   3   4   5

12. Please respond to the following questions solely as they relate to the mentoring program you participated during the 2006–2007 school year.

1 = Strongly disagree; 2 = Disagree somewhat; 3 = Agree somewhat; 4 = Agree; 5 = Agree strongly

The mentoring experience was beneficial to my professional experience.

1   2   3   4   5

The knowledge and skills acquired through the mentoring experiences were relevant to improved student performance.

1   2   3   4   5

The options to interact with my mentor were appropriate.

1   2   3   4   5

The mentoring experience helped me to acquire skills needed to comply with the Individuals with Disabilities Education Act (IDEA).

1   2   3   4   5

The mentoring process helped me to become a better teacher.

1   2   3   4   5

The mentoring process was an important component of my professional development.

1   2   3   4   5

13. Would you like to continue support next year?
☐ Yes
☐ No. If no, please explain why:

14. Would you like continuing support from your current mentor?
☐ Yes
☐ No. If no, please explain why:

15. Do you think each new teacher should have a mentor?
☐ Yes
☐ No

16. As a new special education teacher this year, what is the one area in which you felt you could have used more professional development to have made your first year even more successful?

17. I thought the newsletter and e-mail communication kept me informed of upcoming events.
    □ Yes
    □ No

18. The mentoring program made a huge difference in my teaching as a beginning teacher. Please explain why.
    □ Yes
    □ No

19. Did you attend the October 2006 Building Partnerships Kick-Off?
    □ Yes
    □ No

20. Which professional development did you attend that was sponsored by the mentoring program?
    □ Compliance
    □ Accommodations
    □ Inclusion
    □ Small Professional Learning Communities
    □ Literacy

21. What did you find most beneficial from district support?

22. During the 2006–2007 school year, when did you attend professional development?
    □ During school hours
    □ After school hours
    □ Saturday
    □ Summertime
    □ Other, please specify:

23. Please check your preference for attending professional development:
    □ During school hours
    □ After school hours
    □ Saturday
    □ Summertime
    □ Other, please specify:

Source: Gudwin/Salazar-Wallace, Intellectual Property of Miami-Dade County Public Schools, Office of Professional Development.

APPENDIX 6.2: INTERVIEW QUESTION GUIDE

Directions: The researcher will introduce herself and explain the purpose of the study. She will thank participants for taking the time for this informal conversation and encourage them to ask any questions during the interview and express their feelings openly. The researcher will reassure participants that their identity will not be used in any reports.

1. What was your position during the 2006–2007 school year?

2. What grade levels do you teach?

3. During the 2006–2007 school year, you participated in a mentoring program. Please tell me a little about your experience in this program.

4. How do you think the mentoring program impacted your teaching practices?

5. Can you share an example of an instructional activity that you learned how to do from the mentor, each other, professional development, or the support staff?

6. What mentoring activities did you like most? Can you tell me a little more about why you liked those activities?

7. During the program, you participated in classroom visitations. What feedback that you received influenced your teaching practice?

8. How was the mentoring experience beneficial to your professional experience?

9. What early experiences influenced your career decision?

10. How has your family influenced your career goals?

11. What do you see as the greatest barrier and greatest facilitator to achieving your career objectives?

APPENDIX 6.3: PROJECT GATE (GETTING ASSISTANCE FOR TEACHING EFFECTIVELY) 2006–2007 SCHOOL YEAR

The mentoring relationship provides the beginning special education (SPED) teacher with an opportunity to work closely with and learn from an experienced SPED teacher. The mentoring relationship is shaped by the activities in which the mentee and mentor participate together. Structured time set aside is a necessary part of the mentoring relationship as it enables mentoring activities such as observation, co-teaching, and lesson planning to take place. Participation in professional learning communities (PLCs) among the teams is critical.

Beginning Teacher Requirements

1. Participants must attend the four full-day professional development (PD) sessions in order to receive master plan points (refer to your At-a-Glance Calendar). The Project GATE professional development opportunities are specifically designed for you and provide vital information on topics that are relevant to you during your first year and are reflective of your needs as noted on the application page.

2. Communicate with your mentor via telephone or e-mail on a biweekly basis (or more often as needed) and complete and submit Project GATE Communication Log by the end of each month (October, November, December, January, February, March, April, and May).

3. Communicate with your mentor to establish a date and location for four (4) face-to-face collaborations: October/November, December/January, February/March, and April; submit a face-to-face collaboration log by November, December, February, and April.

4. Set up two (2) school-site visitations to your mentor's classroom: December and February. Please contact your mentor's principal to confirm date of visitation. Complete the mentee school-site visitation log. Include in your log a reflective piece. The reflections should identify new concepts you have learned and the specific ways you intend to apply them in the classroom:

   • What I did:

   • What I learned:

   • What I think and feel about this:

   • What it means in my classroom:

- What connections did I make today?

- What would I like to add to my classroom in the way of resources and strategies?

- What changes would I need to make in my instruction?

- What help do I need to put these ideas into effect?

- What I can do:

5. Fax your substitute form by the end of December and February and keep a copy for your records in the Project GATE binder that was provided to you.

6. One of the most important aspects of Project GATE is that each participant grows, not only as a teacher, but also as one who continues being a lifelong learner. Consider how you will continue to grow as an effective teacher.

Dear Colleagues,

We welcome you to our Project GATE family! We have compiled a meaningful and worthwhile program for you. ☺ Please join us in our commitment to increase student achievement by being the most effective teachers.

Thank you for being an integral part of this family,

Denise and Magda

The main factor that really affects student achievement is the effectiveness of the teacher.

—Harry Wong

Source: Gudwin/Salazar-Wallace, Intellectual Property of Miami-Dade County Public Schools, Office of Professional Development.

APPENDIX 6.4: SAMPLE SPECIAL EDUCATION MENTOR TEACHER APPLICATION

Yes, I am interested in participating as a mentor teacher for Project GATE.

Name: _____

Employee #: _____

School name: _____

Work loc. #: _____

School phone: _____

Fax: _____

E-mail: _____

What is your current teaching position?

Specify exceptionality, grade level, and subjects taught.

Do you have national board certification?

Have you been involved in any previous mentoring programs? If so, explain.

What is your area of expertise?

Have you taken the Clinical Education Training or any mentor coaching training? If so, please explain.

Note: Mentors will be contacted for an interview to be held on *Wednesday, September 20, 2006.* A professional development session for mentor teachers will be held on *Saturday, October 7, 2006.* Attendance at the session is mandatory.

Principal's name: _____

Principal's authorization: _____

Contact number: _____

Signature: _____

Application deadline: Friday, September 15, 2006

Source: Gudwin/Salazar-Wallace, Intellectual Property of Miami-Dade County Public Schools, Office of Professional Development.

APPENDIX 6.5: SAMPLE SPECIAL EDUCATION NEW AND EARLY-CAREER TEACHER APPLICATION

Yes, I am interested in participating as a mentee teacher in the Project GATE Mentoring Program.

Name: _____

Employee #: _____

School name: _____

Work loc. #: _____

School phone: _____

Fax: _____

E-mail: _____

What is your current teaching position?

Specify exceptionality, grade level, and subjects taught.

How many years have you taught special education?

Have you been involved in any previous mentoring programs? If so, explain.

In what areas would you be interested in receiving mentoring?

How did you complete your special education certification requirements?

Note: A professional development session for beginning teachers will be held on *Saturday, October 7, 2006.* Attendance at this session is mandatory.

Principal authorization: _____

Contact number: _____

Application deadline: Thursday, September 14, 2006

Source: Gudwin/Salazar-Wallace, Intellectual Property of Miami-Dade County Public Schools, Office of Professional Development.

APPENDIX 6.6: PROJECT GATE 2006–2007 YEARLY CALENDAR AT-A-GLANCE

PROJECT GATE   2006–2007 SCHOOL YEAR

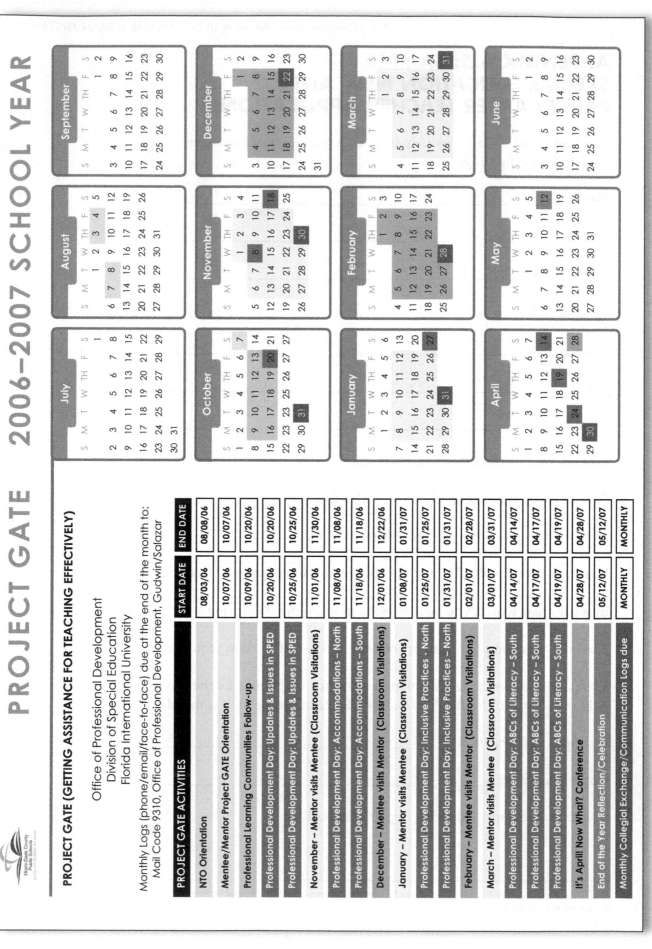

PROJECT GATE (GETTING ASSISTANCE FOR TEACHING EFFECTIVELY)

Office of Professional Development
Division of Special Education
Florida International University

Monthly Logs (phone/email/face-to-face) due at the end of the month to:
Mail Code 9310, Office of Professional Development, Gudwin/Salazar

PROJECT GATE ACTIVITIES	START DATE	END DATE
NTO Orientation	08/03/06	08/08/06
Mentee/Mentor Project GATE Orientation	10/07/06	10/07/06
Professional Learning Communities Follow-up	10/09/06	10/20/06
Professional Development Day: Updates & Issues in SPED	10/20/06	10/20/06
Professional Development Day: Updates & Issues in SPED	10/25/06	10/25/06
November – Mentor visits Mentee (Classroom Visitations)	11/01/06	11/30/06
Professional Development Day: Accommodations – North	11/08/06	11/08/06
Professional Development Day: Accommodations – South	11/18/06	11/18/06
December – Mentee visits Mentor (Classroom Visitations)	12/01/06	12/22/06
January – Mentor visits Mentee (Classroom Visitations)	01/08/07	01/31/07
Professional Development Day: Inclusive Practices – North	01/25/07	01/25/07
Professional Development Day: Inclusive Practices – North	01/31/07	01/31/07
February – Mentee visits Mentor (Classroom Visitations)	02/01/07	02/28/07
March – Mentor visits Mentee (Classroom Visitations)	03/01/07	03/31/07
Professional Development Day: ABCs of Literacy – South	04/14/07	04/14/07
Professional Development Day: ABCs of Literacy – South	04/17/07	04/17/07
Professional Development Day: ABCs of Literacy – South	04/19/07	04/19/07
It's April! Now What? Conference	04/28/07	04/28/07
End of the Year Reflection/Celebration	05/12/07	05/12/07
Monthly Collegial Exchange/Communication logs due	MONTHLY	MONTHLY

Source: Gudwin/Salazar-Wallace, Intellectual Property of Miami-Dade County Public Schools, Office of Professional Development.

7

Professional Development Through Learning Opportunities

When teachers talk about their reasons for doing things and respond to questions about their perceptions and teaching decisions, they often experience a sense of professional excitement and renewed joy and energy related to their work.

—Arthur Costa and Robert J. Garmston (1994)

As you read Chapter 7, we encourage you to reflect upon the following questions:

1. What is critical in designing and planning an effective professional development?

2. What do we need to know regarding diversity of our teachers?

3. What other type of professional development is effective besides workshops?

4. What do I need to know about what adults want and need in their learning?

To help you discover our own understandings of these questions, the content of the chapter is organized in the following sections: Professional Development, Professional Development That Embraces Diversity, Facilitating Adult Learning Opportunities Effectively (including "Never Evers" and adult learning needs), Study Groups, Instructional Data Discussions, Professional Learning Communities, Quality, and Personal and Professional Growth. We anchor the content in the context of various scenarios that illustrate effective professional development.

Debbie is a veteran teacher and one of our eighty-nine mentors who attended an optional, Saturday all-day workshop. Our goal was to provide support in many different formats, from communication via e-mail, phone calls, and newsletters, to learning communities, full-day workshops, and visitation to classrooms. Surprisingly, the Saturday workshop was full of participants ready for a full day of learning, from 8:15 to 3:15, held at a hosting elementary school. Debbie shared in an e-mail written to us the day following the professional development:

Thanks for the great workshop yesterday. I have to tell you—I wasn't crazy about giving up a Saturday, but I felt that I had made the commitment to the program. Anyway, I was pleasantly surprised. It is rare to come away from a workshop feeling as though I've gotten something out of it. I'm usually counting the minutes until it's time to leave. This workshop was great and I hope we can have more. It was so nice to have a chance to just talk to so many really good and caring teachers.

What Debbie may not have recognized was that the small-group discussions and group activities engaged the learners using best-practice professional development strategies. Additionally, the content of the day was targeted on meaningful, worthwhile literacy strategies, which were practical and effective. Debbie was a veteran teacher who welcomed the support and information, but had high expectations and wanted it to be worth her while. . . . Isn't that what every teacher deserves?

As we become more sensitive to the increasing groups of diverse teachers and students in both urban and nonurban settings, we need to target our professional learning opportunities offered to our teachers. Diversity comes to us in many ways, culturally, linguistically, ethnically, academically, socially, and emotionally. How can our professional development meet all of the needs of our teachers, who may be as diverse as their learners, or the opposite, a group that lacks diversity? As Lindsey, Jungwirth, Pahl, and Lindsey (2009) stated so well, "Diversity is prevalent in our society. We cannot *not* have diversity" (p. 75). Additionally, intensive professional development must be designed so that teachers have the opportunity to increase their skills. Our goal for professional development with our group of new teachers included classroom management, instructional practices in literacy, compliance and policies, reflective practice, and utilization of accommodations to meet the needs of diverse learners (i.e., English language learners and students with disabilities). Those topics have been identified by Billingsley (2005) as critical in addressing the needs of mentor teacher leaders and those of new teachers. Since we also found some of the topics in the "needs" list of our mentors and mentees, we provided learning opportunities targeted to their needs and in a variety of formats, including large groups, small groups, and professional learning communities, as well as some individualized unique settings of visiting model classrooms.

PROFESSIONAL DEVELOPMENT

Professional development for mentors as teacher leaders is critical for the success of a program that is designed to support new teachers. "Appropriate training in the role of a mentor is as important as careful selection of the mentor. Mentors are not successful by virtue of their appointment. Successful mentors develop over time through good training, opportunities to share experiences with others, and feedback from supervisors and protégés" (Brock & Grady, 2007, p. 86). Providing professional development to our mentors was a thoughtful process, as was professional development for our new teachers. Ideally, including ongoing learning opportunities in effective coaching and mentoring and providing opportunities to meet with other mentors to share successes and troubleshooting strategies are sound professional development strategies for mentors, teacher leaders, and instructional coaches. The "big buckets" of learning opportunities provided to our mentor teacher leaders included communication skills, effective listening, building trust, observing through the lens of the new teacher's eyes, coaching skills, examining student work, working with adult learning theory, and corrective feedback, all topics that we found to be critical in addressing with our mentor teacher leaders.

> I made wonderful connections with other mentors, and I was able to share and listen to their ideas and build rapport. Everyone's positive attitude inspired me today. There was not room for negativity. In collaborating with other teachers, I was able to learn new teaching ideas and reflect on how to use them in my classroom as well. . . . This is helping me build a wider network of fellow teachers.
>
> —Kathleen Zaldivar, mentor teacher leader

PROFESSIONAL DEVELOPMENT THAT EMBRACES DIVERSITY

Attending professional development as a team in the areas of methods of instruction, content, and compliance was also beneficial, to assist the teacher leader in staying on the same page as the new and early-career teacher, which enables follow-up to be consistent with what was learned. Taking into consideration the culturally heterogeneous diversity of the groups, professional development needs to be a mix of individualistic and collectivistic strategies, using both as a basis for planning a professional development. For example, some people, such as Latino groups, may feel more comfortable with group activities, feeling strength from sharing within a social group, while others may feel more comfortable with working independently on some activities (Rothstein-Fisch & Trumbull, 2008). In taking professional learning opportunities a step deeper, Singleton and Linton (2006) suggest courageously talking about race and establishing a learning community within the school, where staff can develop skills and knowledge to assist them in improving student performance and eliminating racial achievement disparities. They suggest having "four agreements of courageous conversation: (1) stay engaged, (2) experience discomfort, (3) speak your truth, and (4) expect and accept non-closure," which will "allow educators to engage, sustain, and deepen interracial dialogue" (pp. 58–59). "While educators of color often have the knowledge about their own racial experience, they may lack an understanding of how to advance interracial dialogue in a productive way" (Singleton & Linton, 2006, p. 55). As we take a look at the intercultural aspects of professional learning, reflect upon Delpit (1995) and her belief that minority educators believe their "voices to be unheard, their concerns unheeded" and that there is a need to

> collect those voices and concerns in order to assist those of us in teacher education to better address the needs of preservice and inservice teachers of color. It is my hope as well that the finding will provide insights into how to better prepare those from the larger culture to teach the increasingly diverse student bodies they are likely to face in the course of their career. (p. 107)

At times, cultural sensitivity to the individual needs of a diverse partnership may even come naturally with pairs who are exposed to diversity on a day-to-day basis.

FACILITATING ADULT LEARNING OPPORTUNITIES EFFECTIVELY

In addition to the traditional conversations about diversity, during professional development to our mentors and mentees, we followed Peggy Sharp's (1992) "Never Evers of Workshop Facilitation," including a few of our personal favorites, shown in Table 7.1.

Another bit of practical professional development knowledge is from Fogarty and Pete (2004), including ten tips to keep in mind when planning for adult learners and targeting how they learn.

1. "I hope this isn't a waste of my time."

2. "Is this practical?"

3. "Can I use this right away?"

4. "How does this fit for me?"

5. "Who says? Who says this is better?"

6. "Show me how!"

7. "I want an expert."

8. "I wanna look this up on my own."

9. "I'm here with a colleague."

10. "I already know this!"

Table 7.1 The Never Evers of Workshop Facilitation

Never Evers of Workshop Facilitation	Transfer of Knowledge
Never ever require individuals to participate.	We realize that some individuals in a diverse group may be uncomfortable with certain activities, so we remembered to accept their choice of engagement.
Never ever say that you are going to rush through and compress material in order to complete what is usually a longer workshop in a shorter length of time.	We didn't want them to feel cheated, so we thoughtfully planned a series of yearlong professional development opportunities, with flexibility to revise as needs of teachers became evident.
Never ever read a lengthy prepared text.	We understand that diverse participants need to be engaged. We provided a copy for them if it was important, as a resource for reference.
Never ever talk to participants as if they are children.	We made sure that we treated our diverse participants as adults, with respect, in awareness of their cultural, linguistic, social, or emotional needs.
Never ever forget that individuals at the workshop are unique, with needs, interests, and experiences particular to them.	Our goal was to always respect and inspire our participants. We tuned in to the needs of our diverse population, both as individuals and as a group.

Source: Adapted from Sharp (1992).

All of the above common comments should be considered when planning professional learning opportunities for both new teachers and mentors. We must listen to the voices of our participants! These typical comments will assist us in planning more effective professional development.

Fogarty and Pete (2007) further describe "rich, robust, and rigorous models of professional learning" (p. 41) as having seven critical qualities that should be considered when planning and providing professional development: (1) sustained—professional development is implemented over time; (2) job embedded—either occurs or is followed up at the work site; (3) collegial—builds and supports a community of learners; (4) interactive—engages learners; (5) integrated—eclectic, meaning face-to-face, online, and so forth; (6) results oriented—does it work and do we see results because of it? and (7) practical or hands-on—teachers need to see how it can work for them. By focusing on these seven qualities of effective professional development during the planning stages, the results will be evident. According to Cramer, Gudwin, and Salazar (2007), the objective of collegial interaction in learning communities is that "follow-up, assessment, and adjustment of instruction result in internal expertise that is then shared by a group of teachers" (p. 15). Schmoker (2006) describes this as imperative to effective professional development. "Teacher support, which includes collegial interactions, is an effective strategy for increasing teacher performance" (quoted in Cramer, Gudwin, & Salazar, 2007, p. 15). Our goal was to lead our teachers to "sustained implementation of new teaching practice in schools" as Knight (2007, p. 26) suggests, and we were able to achieve it by planning out the year of professional development and communication, based on the needs of our teachers.

We found that when our teachers built and maintained trust, respect, and friendships among themselves, a bond was developed between learners that provided a boost for implementation. This was evident in our community of learners throughout Project GATE, the mentoring program in our case study. The bonds formed as partners were provided outside support through professional development and learning communities, and as the partnerships grew, so did the camaraderie within the groups. Ongoing communication through our e-mails and newsletters also kept this bond strong. As mentors become more knowledgeable in working with other adults, our goal was to increase coaching skills.

> This is a terrific venue for collaborative discourse between teachers. The greatest component is that both teachers learn and as a result become better at their profession.
>
> —Liana, mentor teacher leader

It was a reciprocal venture. According to Robbins (2004), "Many mentors believe that mentoring has made them more effective and conscious of their own practices and their consequences" (p. 150). This type of professional development does not occur only in workshops.

> Learning is an ongoing process, and this experience of being a mentor has been a learning experience for me. . . . I have learned a lot about myself as a teacher and as an individual.
>
> —Evelys, mentor teacher leader

Professional development that connects newly learned concepts to prior knowledge should include knowledge base, demonstration, time to reflect, and time for practice with feedback (Robbins, 2004). Coaching and mentoring are skills to achieve, but nurturing that goal takes time and extensive professional development. As part of the professional development venue, study groups, data chats, and professional learning communities are job-embedded learning opportunities in which the mentor and new teacher may be able to participate together.

STUDY GROUPS

Let's look at study groups as another effective method for the instructional coach to utilize, which includes wearing the hat of the coach and mentor as a learning facilitator.

> It's 2:15 p.m. and Yessi, a young, energetic, Cuban American teacher, is anxiously awaiting her study group meeting. With file folder in tote, she hurries to the teacher's lounge. Her study group will begin its weekly meeting. In her folder, she finds some of the protocols and a few articles that the facilitator has provided. Yessi's study group includes six teachers of various cultural and linguistic backgrounds. Yessi is excited because this group has provided her with specific teaching strategies to utilize with her struggling readers. It has also given her the opportunity to build a stronger bond with her coach, Samina, a teacher of Pakistani descent. The group begins the session by reflecting on the essential question driving their work that was posed by Dakota, a Midwestern exemplary teacher whose turn it is to facilitate. The group engages in meaningful conversation regarding the chapter they studied from a book on vocabulary development and reading comprehension. Discussions take place regarding student work, and as a group, they analyze achievement data in order to move the struggling readers forward. Yessi takes notes as they exchange ideas and teaching experiences. The study group concludes, and Samina and Yessi walk back to their classrooms while planning how to use the newly learned strategies in Yessi's classroom.

In reflecting on her experience in study groups, Yessi says,

> Without the support of other teachers engaging in meaningful work, and without having been given the opportunity to analyze my own students' work in vocabulary development and reading comprehension together, I could not have possibly become as skillful in the classroom with my students as I did.

In collaboration with Samina, the instructional coach provided to support her through her first year of teaching, Yessi found participating in study groups a worthwhile experience.

Yessi and Samina participated in study groups together, which is a job-embedded professional learning opportunity, formed by instructional staff members, who meet according to their grade levels, departments, or as indicated by individual school needs. The purpose of study groups is to increase student achievement. Each group begins with the analysis of student data, then they design an action plan indicating what the students' needs are, as well as what they will do when the group meets, in order to continue their quest of improving student achievement. Study groups engage in meaningful conversation and informal research. Teachers need to have professional learning experiences that are flexible, focused, and responsive to both their needs and the needs of their students. According to Murphy (2001), study groups are embedded in five fundamental principles, about which Yessi shared, "*The principles behind study groups are fantastic and should be implemented in all schools. Study groups helped me as a beginning teacher. I implemented the concept behind study groups with my own students in my classroom.*"

Look at the five principles of study groups in Table 7.2. Reflect upon how this type of learning opportunity might enhance your own experiences.

Table 7.2 Five Principles of Study Groups

	Principles	*How It Was Demonstrated in Real Life*
1	Students are first: The first step in organizing study groups is founded on the concept that the students' needs are considered first. What do the students need in order to achieve?	Yessi and Samina's group brought in the charted data based on monthly assessments for data charts, keeping in mind that the students were the focus.
2	Everyone participates: All members engage in meaningful discussions.	The group highlighted their individual class strengths in instruction and also an area needing assistance at each meeting.
3	Leadership is shared: All members take turns in facilitating the group.	Yessi took a turn to facilitate on the third meeting. Although it was a bit scary, it helped her build confidence as she led the group.
4	Responsibility is equal: All members take responsibility for the work that is being accomplished by the group.	The group equally divided the tasks to be completed before the next meeting.
5	The work is public: The logs and notes, as well as action plans, are shared with other groups.	Yessi and Samina's group maintained a blog online.

Source: Adapted from Murphy (2001).

INSTRUCTIONAL DATA DISCUSSIONS

The role of the instructional coach includes participating in discussions that revolve around various data, reviewing and analyzing, working together to plan for what the data mean in terms of instructional change, and may include observing classroom practices, modeling lessons, planning, and co-teaching. The "data coach" becomes a lifeline connecting the data (which oftentimes can be a daunting task) to high-quality instructional practices.

Suzy is very comfortable in analyzing data. Her special education background has paved the road for her success, given the sheer numbers of student data she has worked with over the years. She is eager to share her knowledge with her beginning teacher, Tisha, who has little experience in reviewing the numerous data points that she is expected to know about. Tisha is lost. She admits that all of the data is swirling around in her head and she doesn't know what to do with any of it. Suzy and Tisha sit down at the public library one Saturday morning after breakfast, and Suzy spreads out all the information on a table. She demonstrates how she organizes it in like-piles. They "Post-it note" the data by prioritizing each piece according to its effectiveness. They add the information to a chart that Suzy created to organize the information and graph it out so it is visually represented. "Oh . . . this is making sense! I see it now." Tisha is making the connections needed to expand data to instructional practice. Suzy, the mentor, has worn the data coach hat and has made great strides working together with Tisha.

PROFESSIONAL LEARNING COMMUNITIES

"Learning communities by their very nature are issues-based, reflective, diverse, and interconnected through inquiry" (Lindsey, Jungwirth, Pahl, & Lindsey, 2009, p. 129) and are a way of building capacity for increased conversations, zeroing in on specific areas of teaching and learning. Instructional coaches and their new teachers may choose to participate in a professional learning community (PLC) together as another successful and effective component of peer coaching. Participants of the PLC play various roles. Besides having a facilitator, PLCs have a "presenter," while another acts as the "process" observer and keeps notes as to how the learning community is working. Protocols are often used and highly recommended to effectively guide the discussions. A PLC meets on a sustained, regular basis to problem solve together as a group of individuals who have similar goals. Students are the core focus of their work. One of the models for effective PLCs may look like this:

1. During the first meeting, the norms are set. Ground rules can be established by asking each individual in the group to write one thing that they need in order to work productively in a group (such as, to start on time, avoid cancellations, etc.). Each rule is written up for all the members to review. If some of the participants cannot abide by the rules, the group discusses and reaches consensus. The group then accepts these as the ground rules for the learning community and reviews them as needed to refocus the learning community.

2. The learning community then engages in structured conversation guided by the presenter (usually about thirty minutes long), focusing on an agreed-upon text to build the groups' common language and understanding.

3. The learning community then engages in structured conversation through the use of a protocol, for about thirty minutes, regarding

the information presented. Debriefing and reflecting on the work together is critical to this structured conversation and can either be embedded within the thirty minutes or be presented as an additional ten minutes at the end of the discussion.

4. Finally, the learning community spends approximately fifteen minutes planning for the next meeting.

Lindsey, Jungwirth, Pahl, and Lindsey (2009) challenge us to use the learning community as an opportunity to ask "breakthrough questions," using "language that redirects thinking away from certainty and asking 'What's wrong?' to curiosity and asking 'What's possible?'" (p. 67). They also encourage us to reflect on how to "promote unity and individuality" by combining the cultures of grade levels with "shared beliefs, values, and vision for the school" (p. 78).

When teachers engage in PLCs, they pool knowledge and increase their capabilities in reaching and working with all students. They create and add to their "teacher toolbox." This deepens their own understanding of what they need to learn and how to make changes in their practice.

INTERNET RESOURCES FOR FURTHER INFORMATION

http://www.nsrfharmony.org/resources.html for resources

http://www.nsrfharmony.org/protocol/protocols.html for samples of protocols to use

http://wwww.sedl.org/pubs/change34 for general information

http://www.hsalliance.org/hsallianceresources.asp for general information

---

We recommend that these three job-embedded learning structures for inquiry and application be interwoven with effective coaching and mentoring, for a positive contribution to the learning outcomes of not only the new and early-career teachers, but their mentors as well.

QUALITY

In general, the work of Joyce and Showers (2002) and Fogarty and Pete (2007) can be a beacon of light in the world of quality professional development for educators. As discussed previously in Chapter 4 (Table 4.1), Joyce and Showers (2002) compare the percentage of teachers' attainment of skills in four areas: (1) theory presented (15% teacher accomplishment and realization), (2) modeling of skills (18% teacher accomplishment and realization), (3) opportunity for practice and low-risk feedback (80% teacher accomplishment and realization), and (4) coaching and study teams (90% teacher accomplishment and realization). Coaching and study teams, as a follow-up to workshops, are methods of quality professional development.

We found that the quality of professional development offered to both our mentors and "their" new teachers was paramount.

> In-class support in the form of coaching, practice, and feedback, provides teachers with a support model, whereby teachers have someone to lean on and from whom to learn, taking the workshop format of professional development into a new dimension of teacher-skill attainment. Increasing teacher performance (with a goal of increasing student achievement) is possible through professional development, which must consist of teacher support. (Cramer, Gudwin, & Salazar, 2007, p. 14)

We used what we learned from previous research to build the professional development segment for this mentoring program. It is obviously critical to provide professional learning opportunities in the way of coaching and study teams whenever possible, coupled with opportunities for practice and feedback. We were able to combine these with workshop models to effectively make a difference in the teaching practices of our new teachers and their mentors.

According to Robbins (2004), professional development that connects newly learned concepts to prior knowledge should include knowledge base, demonstration, time to reflect, and time for practice with feedback. In fact, when reflecting, Maria, a new teacher who came to the field of education as a second career, summed up the mentoring experience as related to the professional development offered as beneficial:

> It was my building block. It was my foundation. It also made me more aware of special education. It made me more conscious of what I wanted to do. . . . The mentoring program encouraged me to seek other things, than just going to a job. It made me realize that it was a profession, a love for a field. So, it made me a better person.

PERSONAL AND PROFESSIONAL GROWTH

As teachers obtain knowledge from professional development, it is our hope that both new teachers and mentors are able to utilize their new knowledge and incorporate it into their own personal and professional growth. As Barbara, one of our unique "new" teachers—one who had taught for many years in one area, but felt brand new again with a new teaching assignment in a class for autism, a totally different class in special education from what her previous experiences were—shares,

> I was also introduced to the Council for Exceptional Children and began to explore new avenues and professional development

through that. And even got involved with the Florida Council for Exceptional Children with the state conference this year. Through this mentoring program, I was able to begin a development program of myself. . . . After every meeting [professional development], I always felt empowered and I felt like I had a real vigor in me that I could go back and implement all the things that I learned. . . . We worked a lot as a team, the team work is incredible.

Through high-quality professional learning opportunities, effective expansion of personal and professional growth occurs. We agree with Joyce and Showers (2002): The challenge is for all of us—teachers, school-site and central office administrators, policy-makers (and we would like to add university systems)—to "put in place a staff development system that nurtures learning communities, injects new knowledge and life into classrooms, and engages students in increasingly successful learning experiences" (p. 10). Isn't that what every teacher *and* every student deserve?

8

Lessons Learned

It is one of the most beautiful compensations of this life that no man can sincerely try to help another without helping himself.

—Ralph Waldo Emerson

As you read Chapter 8, we encourage you to reflect upon the following questions:

1. How does a mentoring program affect student achievement?

2. How can a university implement lessons learned from the mentoring and support programs in school districts in their own preservice teacher preparation programs?

3. How can a school district apply what has been learned to planning and implementing support activities for new teachers?

4. What can be learned and replicated in individual school districts?

To help you discover your own understandings of these questions, the content of the chapter is organized into our lessons learned, with a focus on these four questions. We anchor the content in the context of two scenarios that illustrate the thoughts of new teachers within an effective mentoring program.

WHAT WE HAVE LEARNED

The lessons we have learned come directly from our involvement with teachers. The feedback from mentees, mentors, and district personnel shaped the teachers' beliefs about teaching practices, shaped who they were as teachers, and improved their instructional approaches. To encourage the reader—whether a teacher, district staff, or a university professor—to reflect on various components of quality induction programs, the preceding four questions are explored.

How Does a Successful Mentoring Program Affect Student Achievement?

We have learned that new teachers who are prepared and supported provide a more effective classroom environment for their students, who in turn are more successful, resulting in an increase in student achievement. We have also learned that mentors who support new teachers also acquire new skills, which results in an increase in student achievement. When teachers form a strong mentoring relationship, share ideas, and work together for a common goal, the reciprocal learning that takes place can be a win-win situation for them and their students.

How Can a University Implement Lessons Learned From the Mentoring and Support Programs in School Districts to Their Own Preservice Teacher Preparation Programs?

During the inception of Project GATE, Florida International University saw the need to connect to the local school system in an effort to combine resources for the success of new teachers. At the beginning of Project GATE, staff from the special education department at the central office level of the school district worked hand in hand with key professors of the university. Later on, these efforts were expanded from only special education to include the office of professional development as well. In the case of Project GATE, state funding was initiated from Florida International University, through the local Council of the Comprehensive System of Personnel Development/ Professional Development Partnerships (Florida International University, 2006) and Miami-Dade County Public Schools, Division of Special Education, combining resources to provide stipends and substitute funding for classroom visits.

This teamwork between the school system and a local university is ideal; when two entities join forces for a common goal, great programs are born. Teamwork should include regular communication, face-to-face meetings, sharing of information, presenting findings, and continuing the dialogue between school system and university. Keeping the support ongoing and nurturing the program through the years are critical components to keeping the program successful. We encourage universities and school districts to work together to support new teachers. It is what our new teachers deserve. It is what their students need.

How Can a School District Apply What Has Been Learned to Planning and Implementing Support Activities for New Teachers?

Many districts have induction programs that are thriving; however, the additional necessary components that we found to be critical for effective success in the planning and implementation include the following:

1. A sincere connection between mentor and new teacher

2. Consistent communication between the program and the participants

3. Ongoing, quality professional development targeting both the needs of the new teachers and the needs of the mentors

4. A go-to, contact person, a liaison to the program, one who also serves as a more generalized mentor to the whole program, with a sense of ownership for its success

5. A team of staff who are knowledgeable, caring, kindhearted, organized, empathetic, and are the type of people who are willing to go the extra mile for their teachers and the program they are spearheading

The combination of these five components brought a sense of belonging for the new teachers.

What Can Be Learned and Replicated in Individual School Districts?

We strongly believe that Project GATE can be replicated and the basic framework, including the collaboration between university and school district, is an ideal beginning. The following eight simple steps for replication may be utilized by large or small districts, urban or rural, with varying school performance levels and differing school populations:

1. Explore collaboration with a local state or private university or other organizations within your region.

2. Choose the target group of new teachers. (Target groups may be subgroups of teachers such as content area, elementary K–5, special education, and so forth, which might be utilized as role-alike learning communities. Some districts may choose to expand the group of new teachers to all newly hired teachers.)

3. Plan how to welcome the new teachers and mentors and how to build those relationships, keeping in mind the five components provided above.

4. Survey the needs of the new teachers and the mentors; needs assessment should be done two or three times a year.

5. Set up the annual goals of the program—what do you want to accomplish?

6. Organize the critically important component of communication by creating:
   a. Annual calendar
   b. Monthly newsletters
   c. Telephone tree
   d. E-mail distribution lists for ongoing e-mail communication

7. Set up professional development topics, dates, locations, and speakers, based on the needs of both the new teachers and the mentors.

8. Continue to build and maintain relationships with both new teachers and mentors, keeping the five necessary components listed above as a focus.

WHAT ARE THE LESSONS LEARNED, AND, JUST AS IMPORTANT, FROM WHOM DID WE LEARN THEM?

The new teachers themselves and their mentors taught us the most about mentoring. As we visited classrooms, spoke with new teachers and their mentors, reviewed teaching methods, provided quality professional development, and followed up with research, we learned that yes indeed, student achievement is impacted by the effectiveness of a new teacher. As part of sharing our lessons learned, we want to spotlight two new teachers, Maria and Cristina, who illustrate the learning that occurred with all of us.

FROM THE VOICES OF TWO TEACHERS

Spotlight on Maria

Maria is an exemplary teacher now in her third year of teaching. She has become a voice for her struggling students, as well as other teachers at her school site.

However, the confidence that Maria exudes now was not as evident during her first year, or even a thought of something that could be possible.

Before becoming a teacher and while working at IVAX Pharmaceuticals, she decided to start university classes to earn a degree in psychology. While applying for a job as a psychologist, she worked as a substitute teacher at her daughter's school, and quickly realized that teaching students was her life calling. During the first few months as a new teacher, while attending a professional development designed for beginning special education teachers, Maria cried, little tears softly rolling down her cheeks, as she quietly lamented to her unbeknownst future mentor from the district office that she was not a good enough teacher to her students. Although she chose the alternative route to teaching, and even though she was very hard on herself and didn't yet possess the confidence in herself as a teacher, she excelled during her first year. Maria was a dedicated beginning second-career teacher, on her way to becoming an exemplary second-career teacher, even though she didn't realize it at first.

Maria reflects on her first year at a school where the student population consists of primarily of Hispanics and black, non-Hispanics:

> *I must admit that choosing the alternative route to a teaching certificate is definitely a challenge. However, I firmly believed that my efforts would profoundly impact my life and that of a child. During the first few weeks of school, I aligned myself with an array of experienced and supportive teachers who guided me to find my strengths as a teacher. Because of this association, I learned about Project GATE. I grabbed at the opportunity to participate in Project GATE (Getting Assistance for Teaching Effectively), a mentoring program provided through the Office of Professional Development and Special Education of our school district. I received mentoring from a veteran teacher, consisting of instruction and much-needed moral and social support. My ability to formulate new theories and teaching strategies directly impacted my students' achievement. Because of this program, my eyes were opened to discover that teachers travel through several phases, including anticipation, survival, disillusionment, rejuvenation, and reflection. Although participating in Project GATE was optional, it was apparent that seeking assistance during my first year of teaching was of the utmost importance.*

Maria dove into her role as an educator and enrolled in a graduate-level cohort program for an autism endorsement, another project jointly sponsored by Florida International University and Miami-Dade County Public Schools. She also agreed to participate on the board of the local chapter of the Council for Exceptional Children (CEC) at our suggestion, giving back to the community—taking on the role of newsletter chair, spearheading the collection of all donations for "goody bags" for children who were recognized as recipients of the Special Education Summer Camp Scholarship Program, and tirelessly offering her help as needed. This involvement led Maria to her role with us as part of the core local committee of the state CEC conference for Florida in 2007. In addition, Maria was awarded the "Teachers as Heroes" Award sponsored by the Dade Reading Council, in recognition of reading activities that engaged her students in becoming lifelong readers; and she was nominated by her peers to represent her school as the Council for Exceptional Children's Rookie Teacher of the Year. In Maria's submission for Rookie Teacher of the Year, she wrote:

(Continued)

(Continued)

Ralph Waldo Emerson once said, "It is one of the most beautiful compensations of this life that no man can sincerely try to help another without helping himself." In helping others through organizations like the Florida Council for Exceptional Children and its local chapter, Miami Chapter 121, I have helped myself to grow professionally. I see beyond each child's disability and focus instead on his strengths to guide him to reach his full potential. I maintain my students' best interests at heart, always. My enthusiasm and passion for teaching are contagious. My keen awareness and understanding of my students allow me to emphasize my belief that each child is unique and special and has the ability to learn.

I consider Project GATE as the springboard to my success in my teaching career. Professional development programs that target beginning teachers should be continuously offered to promote teacher retention. Because of Project GATE and the collaboration with master teachers, I was able to create my own style of teaching and incorporate my enthusiasm and creativity into my lessons.

Spotlight on Cristina

Cristina was an exemplary first-year teacher, whose passion in working with special needs students began when she herself was still in high school, inspired by two exemplary teachers. Her commitment expanded to weekends when she volunteered her time with special students. Another influence in her profession was her mother, who at the time taught immigrant students who were struggling to learn English. In the words of Cristina:

Fortunately Project GATE rescued me. I was paired up with one of the most knowledgeable teachers for trainable mentally handicapped students in the district. I still to this day collaborate with her for special projects and for advice. My mentor taught me how to create wonderful IEPs, what items should be brought to parents' attention during an IEP, as well as how to address certain parents. For that I'm ever grateful. I learned how to spread my wings in order to have a deeper impact on my students. I became more involved with local community agencies such as City of Hialeah Special Populations, Special Olympics, Best Buddies, Shake-A-Leg, and Council for Exceptional Children. [Cristina was also nominated by her peers as Rookie Teacher of the Year. According to a colleague, "Ms. Ugalde's dedication toward her athletes in Special Olympics was the reason they performed so successfully and were awarded several medals. For her first year sponsoring Best Buddies, the club was fortunate enough to have record membership. Once again she collaborated with another teacher to take ten students who were trainable mentally handicapped, along with their Best Buddies, to Walt Disney World. It was an experience the students will never forget. It was truly a trip of their dreams."] Currently I'm aspiring to attend a local university to start coursework for a Specialist Degree in Leadership and Administration. I would like to become a better advocate for these kids at a more in-depth level, district or preferably state level. I learned to join the tech committee, grant committee, and the Educational Excellence School Advisory Council (EESAC) in order to collaborate and exchange ideas with other professionals. Our students deserve the best and need to be viewed as individuals and not as mentally handicapped students. My students have given me the passion and drive to assist in making the positive changes needed to include them in our classroom as well as our society.

Cristina took her students sailing, providing them experiences beyond both her and their wildest dreams. What made this happen? How did that occur? Her mentor, Evelys, an award-winning teacher herself, was involved in the Shake-A-Leg Program and introduced Cristina to new adventures. Her mentor, who became a close friend in the process, assisted Cristina in the process of becoming an even better first-year teacher, while building and maintaining a strong relationship and mentor/teacher bond. Following our suggestion, Cristina also became part of the core planning committee for our state Florida Council for Exceptional Children Conference for 2007. Her involvement in many areas of education provided her with a sense of belonging that enhanced her classroom teaching skills during her first year of teaching.

WHAT ARE THE CONNECTING THREADS WOVEN INTO THE EXPERIENCES OF SUCCESSFUL MENTORING RELATIONSHIPS AND SUCCESSFUL NEW TEACHERS?

First and foremost, there was a sincere, strong connection between mentor and new teacher. That was evident and obvious, as even just a glimpse of Maria and Cristina show. There was consistent communication between the mentor and the new teacher, as well as between the central office staff and the participants. For many of our teams, we also had a sincere, strong connection with one or both of the partners, and that continued to seal their commitment to the project. Both mentors and new teachers participated in ongoing, quality professional development designed for them that targeted each of their needs. A strong relationship was built between the mentors, new teachers, and us (the two go-to, contact persons who were liaisons to the program and who served as additional mentors), which provided a much-needed sense of belonging for both the new teachers and their mentors. Opportunities to get involved with various organizations and collaborative groups or committees were offered by the mentors and also by us, and many of the new teachers jumped to the new prospects and took full advantage of the opportunities. All individuals who were involved in the most successful teams were knowledgeable, caring, kindhearted, organized, empathetic types of people who were willing to go the extra mile for their teachers and the program. Collaboration between university and school district was an added bonus that we highly recommend. These components are needed for a successful mentoring program.

In our research and personal work with mentoring new teachers and mentoring mentors, we have found that the top three keys to success were personal connections, communication, and professional development.

Everything we do as mentors, every little task of mentoring or supporting, assisting or listening, coaching or guiding, is a step toward the success line for our new teachers. As new teachers shared with us frequently, even the small steps can sometimes be overwhelming, and sometimes made possible *only* because there was a lifeline just a whisper away.

> I long to accomplish a great and noble task, but it is my chief duty to accomplish small tasks as if they were great and noble.
>
> —Helen Keller, 1880–1968

Lessons learned: We learned that we must treat each small task as if it is great and noble. We also learned that being that lifeline to our new teachers and to our mentors is what we need to do. We learned that the winners of this journey were all of us—the planning and implementation team, both the new teachers and their mentors. And most important, the real winners were and must always be the students, the core of what we do, the heartbeat of it all.

Glossary of Terms

Bilingual/Biliterate: Ability to speak, read, and write in two languages easily and naturally.

Camaraderieship: A term coined by a teacher who wanted to communicate her desire for comradeship, to experience a form of camaraderie.

Case Study: A type of research approach that includes a systematic way of looking at people and events, as well as data collection, analysis, and reporting of results.

Communication: The process of imparting information, via verbal/spoken language, nonverbal language, such as body language and gestures, and written language. Includes meaning, which is sensitive to cultural inferences, background knowledge, and attending skills.

Culturally and Linguistically Diverse (CLD) Populations: A demographic shift to a more diverse population that includes all backgrounds of culture and language, with components of language, traditions, gestures, family dynamics, and characteristics.

Diversity: Variety, assortment, a mixture.

Induction Programs: Various models utilized throughout districts and states across the nation. Some of the common components include new teacher orientation, induction committee, mentoring, professional development, professional growth plan, and administrative support.

Intercultural: Situations occurring between two or more cultures of people.

Intergenerational: Situations occurring between two or more generations of people.

Instructional Coach: A teacher, mentor, or professional developer who works with and teaches other educators how to use proven instructional methods. To be successful in this role, a coach may wear many "hats" such as exemplary teacher, skillful listener, and trusted friend and confidant.

Mentor: A more experienced person who assists another person, sometimes in the role of a friend, counselor, colleague, or teacher. Many professions have mentoring programs where new persons in the field have a mentor to turn to for advice, to communicate with in time of need, and to ultimately assist them in becoming successful in their field.

Nicaraguana, Nicaraguense: (Spanish) A woman from Nicaragua.

Professional Development: An increase in skill or knowledge, in the form of workshops, mentors, professional learning communities. Sometimes known as staff development.

Professional Learning Communities (PLCs): Groups of educators paired together for learning as a successful type of professional development. PLCs expand the learning opportunities for educators through engaging in cooperative and collaborative learning in the school or district setting.

Teacher Leader: A leadership role for teachers. Often it is a shared leadership role that involves collaboration in the day-to-day workings of a school or district, where the teacher shares expertise in the field to increase student performance and overall school success.

References

Abrams, J. (2008, April 21). *Key skills for instructional coaching and being generationally savvy: Supporting administrators and teachers of all generations.* Presentation to Instructional Coaches, Miami, Florida.

Axtell, R. (1998). *Gestures: The do's and taboos of body language around the world.* New York: John Wiley & Sons.

Billingsley, B. (2005). *Cultivating and keeping committed special education teachers.* Thousand Oaks, CA: Corwin.

Blazer, C. (2006). Teacher transfer and turnover. *Research Capsule, 0601.* Miami, FL: Miami-Dade County Public Schools. Retrieved January 12, 2008, from http://drs.dadeschools.net/informationcapsules/IC.asp.

Bogdan, R., & Bilken, S. (2007). *Qualitative research for education: An introduction to theories and methods.* Boston, MA: Pearson.

Bos, C., & Vaughn, S. (2002). *Strategies for teaching students with learning and behavior problems* (5th ed.). Boston: Allyn & Bacon.

Boyer, K., & Gillespie, P. (2003). *Making the case for teacher retention.* Retrieved August 11, 2009, from http://www.wested.org/nerrc/Acrobat%20Files/KQTsection1MakingCase.pdf.

Brock, B., & Grady, M. (2006). *Developing a teaching induction program: A guide for school leaders.* Thousand Oaks, CA: Corwin.

Brock, B., & Grady, M. (2007). *From first-year to first rate: Principals guiding beginning teachers.* Thousand Oaks, CA: Corwin.

Chamberlain, S., Guerra, P., & Garcia, S. (1999). *Intercultural communication in the classroom.* Austin, TX: Southwest Educational Development Laboratory. (ERIC Document Reproduction Service No. ED432573)

Cochran-Smith, M., & Zeichner, K. (2005). *Studying teacher education: The report of the AERA Panel on Research and Teacher Education.* Mahwah, NJ: Lawrence Erlbaum Associates.

Costa, A., & Garmston, R. (1994). *Cognitive coaching: A foundation for renaissance schools.* Norwood, MA: Christopher-Gordon.

Council for Exceptional Children. (2003). *What every special educator must know: CEC International Standards for Entry into Professional Practice* (6th ed.). Arlington, VA: Author. Retrieved August 12, 2009, from http://www.cec.sped.org/Content/NavigationMenu/ProfessionalDevelopment/ProfessionalStandards/?from=tlc Home.

Council of Chief State School Officers. (2006). *Interstate new teacher assessment and support consortium (INTASC).* Washington, DC: Author. Retrieved March 11, 2007, from http://www.ccsso.org/projects/Interstate_New_Teacher_Assessment_and_Support_Consortium.

Cramer, E., Gudwin, D., & Salazar, M. (2007). Professional development: Assisting urban schools in making annual yearly progress. *Journal of Urban Learning, Teaching, and Research, 3,* 13–24.

Darling-Hammond, L. (1999). Teacher quality and student achievement: A review of state policy evidence. *Education Policy Analysis Archives, 8*(1).

Davis, B. (2007). *How to teach students who don't look like you: Culturally relevant teaching strategies.* Thousand Oaks, CA: Corwin.

Delgado, M. (1999). Lifesaving 101: How a veteran teacher can help a beginner. *Educational Leadership, 56*(8), 27–29.

Delpit, L. (1995). *Other people's children: Cultural conflict in the classroom.* New York: New Press.

DePaul, A. (1998). *What to expect your first year of teaching.* Washington, DC: Office of Educational Research and Improvement (ED). (ERIC Document Reproduction Service No. ED423236)

Dresser, N. (2005). *Multicultural manners: Essential rules of etiquette for the 21st century.* Hoboken, NJ: John Wiley & Sons.

Dunne, K., & Villani, S. (2007). *Mentoring new teachers through collaborative coaching.* San Francisco: WestEd.

Florida Department of Education. (2003). *Florida teacher retention 1992–2002.* Tallahassee, FL: Office of Policy Research and Improvement.

Florida Department of Education. (2007). *Teacher demographics in Florida's public schools, Fall 2006.* Statistical Brief Series 2007–17B. Tallahassee, FL: Bureau of Education Information and Accountability Services.

Florida International University. (2006). *2004–2006 Biennial Report for Florida International University's College of Education.* Miami, FL: Author.

Fogarty, R., & Pete, B. (2004). *The adult learner: Some things we know.* Thousand Oaks, CA: Corwin.

Fogarty, R., & Pete, B. (2007). *From staff room to classroom: A guide for planning and coaching professional development.* Thousand Oaks, CA: Corwin.

Friend, M., & Bursuck, W. (2006). *Including students with special needs: A practical guide for classroom teachers* (4th ed.). Boston: Allyn & Bacon.

Gay, G. (2000). *Culturally responsive teaching: Theory, research, and practice.* New York: Teachers College Press.

Grunberg, J., & Armellini, A. (2004). Teacher collegiality and electronic communication: A study of the collaborative uses of email by secondary school teachers in Uruguay. *British Journal of Educational Technology, 35*(5), 597–606.

Gudwin, D. M. (2002, March). *A qualitative study of the perceptions of six preservice teachers: Implementing oral and written retelling strategies in reading to students with learning disabilities.* Paper presented at annual meeting of the Eastern Educational Research Association, Sarasota, FL. (ERIC Document Reproduction Service No. ED466869)

Ingersoll, R. M. (2001). Teacher turnover and teacher shortages: An organizational analysis. *American Educational Research Journal, 38*(3), 499–534.

Institute Student Mentor Programme. (2007). *Mentoring handbook.* Bombay, India: Indian Institute of Technology. Retrieved December 8, 2008, from http:// gymkhana.iitb.ac.in/~hostels/counselingservice/Mentoring%20handbook%20IIT%20Bombay.pdf.

Irvine, J., & York, D. (1995). Learning styles and culturally diverse students: A literature review. In J. Banks & C. McGee Banks (Eds.), *Handbook of research on multicultural education* (pp. 484–497). New York: Macmillan.

Johnston, J. (2008). *Mentoring graduate students.* Nashville, TN: Vanderbilt Center for Teaching. Retrieved December 8, 2008, from http://www.vanderbilt.edu/cft/resources/teaching_resources/interactions/mentoring_grad.htm.

Joyce, B., & Showers, B. (1995). *Student achievement through staff development.* Alexandria, VA: Association for Supervision and Curriculum Development.

Joyce, B., & Showers, B. (2002). *Student achievement through staff development* (3rd ed.). Alexandria, VA: Association for Supervision and Curriculum Development.

Judson, E., & Lawson, A. (2007). What is the role of constructivist teachers within faculty communication networks? *Journal of Research in Science Teaching, 44,* 490–505.

Kardos, S., & Moore Johnson, S. (2007). *On their own and presumed expert: New teachers' experiences with their colleagues.* Retrieved December 26, 2007, from http://www.tcrecord.org/content.asp?contentid=12812.

Kee, K. (2006). How to say it like a coach. *Teachers Teaching Teachers, 2*(3), 1–3.

Killion, J., & Harrison, C. (2005). Role: Mentor. *Teachers Teaching Teachers, 1*(3), 1–3.

Killion, J., & Harrison, C. (2006). *Taking the lead: New roles for teachers and school-based coaches.* Oxford, OH: National Staff Development Council.

Kliebard, H. (2004). *The struggle for the American curriculum: 1893–1958.* New York: Routledge Falmer.

Knight, J. (2007). Five key points to building a coaching program. *Journal of the National Staff Development Council, 28*(1), 26–31.

Kozol, J. (2005). Confections of apartheid: A stick-and-carrot-pedagogy for the children of our inner-city poor. *Phi Delta Kappan, 87*(4), 265–275.

Lindsey, D., Jungwirth, L., Pahl, J., & Lindsey, R. (2009). *Culturally proficient learning communities: Confronting inequities through collaborative curiousity.* Thousand Oaks, CA: Corwin.

Luekens, M., Lyter, D., & Fox, E. (2004). Teacher attrition and mobility: Results from the teacher follow-up survey, 2000–01. *Education Statistics Quarterly, 6*(3). Retrieved July 23, 2007, from http://www.nces.ed.gov/pubs2004/2004301.pdf.

Mangan, M. (1995). *Building cross-cultural competence: A handbook for teachers.* Springfield: Illinois State Board of Education, Educational Equity Services. (ERIC Document Reproduction Service No. ED420166)

Martinez, R. (n.d.). *Hispanic leadership in American higher education.* Hispanic Association of Colleges and Universities. Retrieved October 3, 2008, from http://www.hacu.net/images/hacu/martinez.pdf.

Marzano, R. (2004). *Building background knowledge for academic achievement.* Alexandria, VA: Association for Supervision and Curriculum Development.

Massey, M. (1980). *The people puzzle: Understanding yourself and others.* Reston, VA: Reston Publishing.

McNeil, P., & Klink, S. (2004). School coaching. In L. B. Easton (Ed.), *Powerful designs for professional learning* (pp. 185–194). Oxford, OH: National Staff Development Council.

Miami-Dade County Public Schools. (n.d.). *Mentoring and induction for new teachers.* Miami, FL: Author

Miami-Dade County Public Schools. (2006a). *Statistical highlights 2005–2006.* Miami, FL: Author. Retrieved August 13, 2009, from http://drs.dadeschools.net/new/StatisticalHighlights/SH0506.pdf.

Miami-Dade County Public Schools. (2006b). *Summary district wide, district and school profiles 2005–2006.* Miami, FL: Author. Retrieved June 3, 2007, from www.oada.dadeschools.net.

Moir, E. (1999). The stages of a teacher's first year. In M. Scherer (Ed.), *A better beginning: Supporting and mentoring new teachers.* Alexandria, VA: Association for Supervision and Curriculum Development.

Moir, E., & Bloom, G. (2003). Fostering leadership through mentoring. *Leadership, 60*(8), 58–60.

Moller, G., & Pankake, A. (2006). *Lead with me: A principal's guide to teacher leadership.* Larchmont, NY: Eye On Education.

Murphy, C. (2001). *Whole faculty study groups: WFSG guiding principles.* Retrieved October 9, 2008, from http://www.murphyswfsg.org/principles.htm.

National Board Professional Teaching Standards. (2006). *Performance-based teaching assessments.* Princeton, NJ: Educational Testing Services.

National Center for Education Statistics. (2005). *Schools and staffing survey.* Retrieved July 1, 2007 from http://nces.ed.gov/pubsearch/pubsinfo.asp?pubid=2005335.

National Community for Latino Leadership. (2001). *Reflecting an American vista: The character and impact of Latino leadership.* Retrieved July 18, 2009, from http://www.latinoleadership.org/research/reports/20010110.html.

National Council for Accreditation of Teacher Education (NCATE). (2006). *What makes a teacher effective? A summary of key research findings on teacher preparation.* Washington, DC: Author. (ERIC Document Reproduction Service No. ED495408)

National Education Association. (2003, September). Who we are, why we teach: A portrait of the American teacher. *NEA Today, 22,* 26–35.

Nevin, A., Harris, K., & Correa, V. (2001). Collaborative consultation between general and special educators in multicultural classrooms: Implications for school reform. In C. Utley & F. Obiakor (Eds.), *Special education, multiple education, and school reform: Components of quality education for learners with mild disabilities* (pp. 173–187). Springfield, IL: Charles C Thomas.

Paige, R. (2004). *A guide to education and No Child Left Behind.* Washington, DC: U.S. Department of Education, Office of the Secretary, Office of Public Affairs.

Pitton, D. E. (2000). *Mentoring novice teachers: Fostering a dialogue process.* Arlington Heights, IL: Starlight Professional Development.

Pitton, D. E. (2006). *Mentoring novice teachers: Fostering a dialogue process* (2nd ed.). Thousand Oaks, CA: Corwin.

Poll shows students prefer to grow up with a career in business. (2005, January 31). *New Orleans CityBusiness.* Retrieved August 12, 2009, from http://findarticles .com/p/articles/mi_qn4200/is_20050131/ai_n10176516.

Protheroe, N. (2003). *The informed educator series: Culturally sensitive instruction.* Arlington: VA: Educational Research Service.

Pugach, M. (2005). Research on preparing general education teachers to work with students with disabilities. In M. Cochran-Smith & K. Zeichner (Eds.), *Studying teacher education: The report of the AERA panel on research and teacher education* (pp. 549–590). Mahwah, NJ: Lawrence Erlbaum.

Robbins, P. (2004). Mentoring. In L. B. Easton (Ed.), *Powerful designs for professional learning* (pp. 149–162). Oxford, OH: National Staff Development Council.

Rothstein-Fisch, C., & Trumbull, E. (2008). *Managing diverse classrooms: How to build on students' cultural strengths.* Alexandria, VA: Association for Supervision and Curriculum Development.

Rubin, H., & Rubin, I. (2005). *Qualitative interviewing: The art of hearing data* (2nd ed.) Thousand Oaks, CA: Sage.

Rutherford, P. (2005). *The 21st century mentor's handbook: Creating a culture for learning.* Alexandria, VA: Just Ask Publications.

Salazar, M., Gudwin, D., & Nevin, A. (2008, Spring). A qualitative study of new/early career special education teacher retention in a multicultural urban setting. *Florida Educational Leadership, 8*(2), 50–56.

Schmoker, M. (2006). *Results now: How we can achieve unprecedented improvements in teaching and learning.* Alexandria, VA: Association for Supervision and Curriculum Development.

Sharp, P. (1992). The "neverevers" of workshop facilitation. *Journal of Staff Development, 13*(4), 38–40. (ERIC Document Reproduction Service No. EJ463335)

Singh, D., & Stoloff, D. (2003, January). *Mentoring faculty of color.* Paper presented at the annual meeting of American Association of Colleges for Teacher Education, New Orleans, LA. (ERIC Document Reproduction Service No. ED474179)

Singleton, G., & Linton, C. (2006). *Courageous conversations about race: A field guide for achieving equity in schools.* Thousand Oaks, CA: Corwin.

Smylie, M. (1994). Redefining teachers' work: Connections to the classroom. *Review of Research in Education, 20,* 129–177.

Stansbury, K., & Zimmerman, J. (2002). Smart induction programs become lifelines for the beginning teacher. *Journal of Staff Development, 23*(4), 10–17.

Stone, D., Patton, B., & Heen, S. (1999). *Difficult conversations: How to discuss what matters most.* New York: Penguin Group.

Toll, C. (2005). *The literacy coach's survival guide: Essential questions and practical answers.* Newark, DE: International Reading Association.

University of Michigan. (2006). *How to mentor graduate students: A guide for faculty at a diverse university.* Retrieved August 12, 2009, from hhttp://www.rackham.umich.edu/downloads/publications/Fmentoring.pdf.

Whitaker, S. D. (2000). What do first-year special education teachers need? *Teaching Exceptional Children, 33*(1), 28–36.

Wong, H. (2001, January 26). *How to be an effective teacher.* Presentation to new teachers, Miami-Dade County Public Schools, Miami, FL.

Wong, H., & Wong, R. (1998). *How to be an effective teacher: The first days of school.* Mountain View, CA: Harry K. Wong Publications.

York-Barr, J., & Duke, K. (2004). What do we know about teacher leadership? Findings from two decades of scholarship. *Review of Educational Research, 74*(3), 255 316.

Zelditch, M. (1990, March). *Mentor roles.* Proceedings of the 32nd annual meeting of the Western Association of Graduate Schools, Tempe, AZ.

INTERNET RESOURCES FOR FURTHER INFORMATION ON PROFESSIONAL LEARNING COMMUNITIES

http://www.hsalliance.org/hsallianceresources.asp (for general information)
http://www.nsrfharmony.org/protocol/protocols.html (for samples of protocols to use)
http://www.nsrfharmony.org/resources.html (for resources)
http://www.sedl.org/pubs/change34 (for general information)

Index

Note: Page references followed by *fig* indicate an illustrated figure; followed by *t* indicate a table.

CORWIN

A SAGE Company

The Corwin logo—a raven striding across an open book—represents the union of courage and learning. Corwin is committed to improving education for all learners by publishing books and other professional development resources for those serving the field of PreK–12 education. By providing practical, hands-on materials, Corwin continues to carry out the promise of its motto: **"Helping Educators Do Their Work Better."**

Lightning Source UK Ltd.
Milton Keynes UK
UKOW07f1130231017

311497UK00005B/98/P